AF599270

HIGH RELIABILITY HEALTHCARE

Applying the Secrets of the Nuclear Navy to Save Patient Lives

Jeffrey "Leno" Kuhlman, MD, MPH
Robert "Navy Bob" Ronscka, DBA

Ballast Books, LLC
www.ballastbooks.com

ISBN: 978-1-962202-85-5

Printed in Hong Kong

Published by Ballast Books
www.ballastbooks.com

For more information, bulk orders, appearances, or speaking requests, please email: info@ballastbooks.com.

TABLE OF CONTENTS

PART FOUR: BEHAVIORS AND SYSTEM PROCESSES

INTRODUCTION

TIME FOR A CHANGE

As the negligent homicide conviction and sentencing of nurse RaDonda Vaught recently unfolded, healthcare workers across the nation watched on with empathy and a dread of making a similar mistake themselves one day.

Vaught's tragic error, which led to the death of seventy-five-year-old Charlene Murphey, occurred at Vanderbilt University Medical Center (VUMC) on December 26, 2017.[1] With two years of experience, Vaught was busy as a float nurse helping other nurses as needed with multiple patients and training an orientee.[2] Murphey, who had been admitted to VUMC due to dizziness and vision loss, was to undergo a positron emission tomography (PET) scan that day. Her physician had ordered her a sedative, Versed, to calm her anxiety prior to the procedure. Since Murphey's primary nurse was occupied, the task of administering the medication fell to Vaught.

When Vaught accessed the automatic dispensing cabinet (ADC) for the appropriate medication, she didn't recognize the drug in the patient's profile by its generic name. Looking for Versed, she overrode the patient's profile and typed "VE" into the computer search, then clicked on the first medication that appeared—vecuronium, a paralytic drug. Without confirming she had the correct medication, either at the ADC or the patient's bedside, and without recognizing the physical differences between the two medications, Vaught gave the vecuronium to Murphey, then left her alone and unmonitored. Murphey died the next day as a direct result of the error.

Though Vaught immediately owned and reported the mistake to her employer, VUMC was not so transparent. The hospital reacted to the event by firing Vaught, negotiating a settlement with the family, hiding the incident from both the public and the state, and recording Murphey's cause of death as "natural causes." The full story didn't come to light until ten months later when an anonymous tip prompted an investigation.

While there's no denying Vaught messed up—as busy, distracted humans inevitably do—the bigger question is how did the system fail? What missing safeguards and contributing factors at VUMC led to such an error?

There were many holes in VUMC's process. For instance, because an upgrade to the medical records at VUMC that year caused continuous slowdowns, nurses were instructed to override the ADC to avoid delays, and they did so on a daily basis.[3] Despite the risks of ignoring the safeguard, VUMC required neither a second set of eyes to confirm medications obtained by override nor medication barcoding at the bedside.

In the *British Journal of Anaesthesia,* Dr. Connor Lusk and her fellow authors write of the tragedy, "RaDonda Vaught did not come to work that day to deliberately contribute to Charlene Murphey's death but was set up to fail by a system that allowed a fatal mistake to happen."[4]

Fatal Mistakes

Sadly, fatal mistakes are not rare in healthcare but an all-too-common occurrence. This became distressingly evident nearly a quarter of a century ago when the US Institute of Medicine warned of a nationwide healthcare crisis. A now-famous report titled *To Err is Human: Building a Safer Health System* called for a radical overhaul of US healthcare to reduce an alarming number of errors, mistakes, and failings that led annually to a huge number of patient injuries and deaths.[5]

In response, a whole cottage industry focused on building high reliability organizations (HROs) quickly developed. Hoping to make American healthcare significantly safer and more reliable, most improvement efforts since then have referred back to the principles of high reliability suggested by Karl Weick and Kathleen Sutcliffe (see Chapter 1). However, as Vaught's story so painfully demonstrates, healthcare has *not* become highly reliable. In fact, it hasn't even come close.

While we put the final touches on *High Reliability Healthcare,* we learned of an alarming report from the Johns Hopkins Armstrong Institute Center for Diagnostic Excellence. It estimated that 371,000 patients die and 424,000 become permanently disabled every year due to misdiagnoses, with a huge number of those errors being preventable. The report claimed that medical providers misdiagnose diseases about 11 percent of the time, with strokes misdiagnosed more than 17.5 percent of the time. Nearly 40 percent of all deaths and permanent disabilities can be traced to the incorrect diagnosis of just five diseases: stroke, sepsis, pneumonia, blood clots, and lung cancer. If medical professionals could reduce diagnostic errors by half in these five categories, the Johns Hopkins report said, we could decrease permanent disabilities and deaths by 150,000 a year.[6]

Such statistics are shocking and heartbreaking and cannot be ignored. We must spend time absorbing such reports and reflecting on how we got to this point. Why haven't we done better?

An Urgent Question

We have witnessed *amazing* developments in technology and artificial intelligence since the arrival of the twenty-first century, but our rates of safety and reliability have barely moved. We also enjoy a wealth of consultants and management strategies, but those, too, have failed to improve our record of success.

We face an urgent question today: Why do we continue to believe that the academic approach we've been chasing high reliability with will work eventually when it hasn't made an appreciable difference in twenty years?

A recent article in *The New England Journal of Medicine* described our problem. It concluded that "adverse events during hospitalization are a major cause of patient harm," not unlike the same problem highlighted more than thirty years ago in the Harvard Medical Practice Study.[7] The *NEJM* study identified "adverse events" in nearly one in four admissions, with approximately one-fourth of those events preventable. "These findings underscore the importance of patient safety and the need for continuing improvement," the report said.[8]

But how can we improve patient safety? And how can we make those improvements continual? We've seen more than enough evidence that the time has come to try something else.

But what could that "something else" be if it's not technology, new management systems, or AI?

An Unlikely Mentor

Both of us have extensive backgrounds in the US Navy. Over our decades there, we gained invaluable knowledge and experience related to safety and reliability.

Jeff is an MD with thirty years of naval medicine experience, sixteen of those years spent caring for US presidents (physician to the forty-fourth president, director of the White House medical unit, White House physician, and senior flight surgeon for Marine One from 1997–2013). Jeff has traveled to more than ninety countries, reviewing their healthcare resources. He currently serves as chief quality and safety officer for America's largest hospital, guiding quality, risk, safety, and transformation.

Bob spent twenty-eight years in the US Navy, where he captained the nuclear submarine USS *Texas* and then served as commodore to Submarine Squadron 7 of the Pacific fleet, the largest nuclear submarine squadron in the world. Dubbed "Navy Bob" by President George W. Bush, he served as the naval aide to the president and carried the "nuclear football." After retiring from the navy, Bob spent four years at AdventHealth as executive director for quality and safety. He now teaches courses on quality, leadership, and policy at the University of Central Florida. It should be noted that there has never been another officer of his seniority, trained in the culture of the nuclear navy, who has been a clinical safety leader within one of our nation's largest hospital systems. His experience uniquely positions him to map the critical differences in safety practices between the nuclear navy and the healthcare industry.

A core part of the message of *High Reliability Healthcare* proposes that the US nuclear navy offers healthcare a treasure trove of insight and experience into how to operate in a *far* safer and more reliable way. While we'll delve into the details in Parts Two and Three of this book, for now it's enough to say that the organizational ecosystem developed by Admiral Hyman G. Rickover three-quarters of a century ago has spared the nuclear navy from suffering *even one* nuclear reactor accident since it launched its first nuclear submarine in 1954. The ecosystem Rickover created has made the nuclear navy the world's most highly reliable organization—and the same concepts that fuel the nuclear navy's incredible success can also transform healthcare into a *truly* safe and reliable enterprise.

Let's Start a Movement

If you've concluded that we want to make a big change, you're right. We've grown weary of seminars that present studies proving we've made no significant progress in making healthcare safer, and then continue to present the old familiar script.

Simply put, we're stuck. More than twenty years ago, as an industry, we turned to a scholarly study designed to investigate how airlines and other organizations could best recover from disasters. We felt desperate to improve our safety and reliability but didn't consider how we could make the findings of that academic study resonate with our frontline personnel.

The result was that it didn't resonate at all. Despite countless conversations occurring at the board, administrative, and supervisory levels, nurses, technicians, support personnel, and even large numbers of physicians never received the memo. But even if they had, the study's academic tone and focus on upper management would have prevented it from making a significant difference to the healthcare delivered on the front lines . . . the very situation we find ourselves in now.

Isn't it time for a change? Isn't it time we became the high reliability organizations that, so far, we've only talked about? Each of us can radically improve our organizational performance by applying a few crucial lessons from the nuclear navy, the most highly reliable organization in the world.

Join Us on a Quick Trip

To help us move in a hope-filled direction, we want to take you on a short journey.

First, we'll review the problem and investigate why Weick and Sutcliffe's principles haven't worked in healthcare. Second, we'll see how the nuclear navy faced a similar need for high reliability and how Admiral Rickover met that need by developing an effective culture, clear expectations, "watchstanding principles," and other key factors. Finally, we will unpack Rickover's solution and suggest how that solution can radically improve healthcare.

Along the way, we will give plenty of examples, showing how a culture of trust and caring in conjunction with well-defined standards make a difference at every level.

We *know* high reliability is possible. We've seen it in the nuclear navy, and we have the blueprint. It's time to truly make high reliability in healthcare a reality.

PART ONE

THE PROBLEM

1

TO ERR IS HUMAN

Imagine that you suffer from a life-threatening medical condition. Would you choose to see a doctor who has a track record of giving the wrong diagnosis and medication, spreading infection, or harming in other ways?

We wouldn't either.

Or imagine you want to take a vacation to a sun-drenched, tropical resort. Would you go by air if you knew that one airliner crashes each day, killing nearly seven hundred passengers?

Again, we would say, "No, thanks."

And yet, millions of Americans each year entrust their care to healthcare organizations that produce very similar outcomes. Consider just a few current examples:

- Medical errors cause an estimated 250,000 deaths in the US annually—the equivalent of two fully-packed 747s crashing every day.[9]
- One in four patients is harmed during hospital stays.[10]
- As many as 80 percent of medical bills contain at least one error; medical billing errors cost American families approximately $500 annually.[11]
- Nearly 80,000 people are killed or seriously harmed from misdiagnosis every year.[12]

- Between 7,000 and 9,000 patients die annually from medication errors.[13]
- According to the World Health Organization, adverse events due to unsafe care are likely one of the ten leading causes of death and disability around the world.[14]

These numbers are alarming and should have long since motivated changes designed to create a safer, more cost-effective, and reliable healthcare system.

The truth is that a healthcare cure *was* proposed at the turn of the last century, boldly promising the advent of a new era for high reliability healthcare. Hospitals, clinics, healthcare systems, and industry leaders all scrambled to adopt and implement the suggested cure. Today, untold numbers of articles, books, consultants, and organizations have arisen to promote essentially the same approach to a safer, more effective healthcare system.

But it clearly hasn't worked. As an industry, we haven't significantly reduced medical errors, decreased adverse events, lowered infection rates, minimized surgical mistakes, or lessened medication blunders. Before we look more closely at why our attempts have failed, let's discuss how we first became aware of our shortcomings and how we arrived at our current situation.

This Must Change

In 1999, the Institute of Medicine published a seminal work that shook up the US healthcare scene. The report, *To Err Is Human: Building a Safe Health System,* spotlighted medical errors as a leading cause of death in the United States. It also revealed their astronomical costs—but perhaps most alarming of all, it said most such errors were preventable.

In response to that report, President Bill Clinton signed the Healthcare Research and Quality Act of 1999. But even before then, he announced four initiatives:

1. The formation of an interagency committee called "the Quality Interagency Coordination Task Force," designed to analyze the report and make recommendations to the vice president within sixty days

2. A call for the government agency administrators of health plans to take steps to reduce medical errors
3. Increased funding of $25 million for the Agency for Healthcare Research and Quality (AHRQ) to improve healthcare quality and prevent medical errors
4. Directions to budget and healthcare officials to include quality and safety initiatives in the 2000 federal budget[15]

Two years later, the US Institute of Medicine issued a follow-up report titled *Crossing the Quality Chasm*. That paper recommended a thorough redesign of the entire US healthcare system, targeting improvements in six dimensions of healthcare: patient safety, care effectiveness, patient-centeredness, timeliness, care efficiency, and equity.[16]

Since the healthcare industry felt desperate to latch onto *something* promising, it embraced both reports with gusto. Both papers turned out to be watershed publications that clearly shifted the prevailing discussions.

The Power of Weick and Sutcliffe

A year before the appearance of *Crossing the Quality Chasm*, an academic paper titled "High Reliability: The Power of Mindfulness in Industry" created its own waves. Many thought it might give us some needed help in healthcare.

Karl E. Weick, the lead author among the paper's three contributors, taught organizational behavior and psychology at the University of Michigan. Since the 1980s, he had studied mindfulness, the practice of thoughtfully engaging with and continually evaluating one's surrounding environment with a view toward making helpful changes appropriate to an ever-changing reality. He used the term "personal enactment" to describe an individual's thoughtful engagement with new circumstances to improve his or her environment. By engaging the problem, he said, one changes both the problem and one's perception of it.

Weick had teamed up to write the article with two others, including Karen Sutcliffe, a professor of business and medicine at Johns Hopkins University who specializes in organizational resilience and reliability. The pair studied the effect that individuals in an organization have on the behavior of others within that organization. They spoke of "collective mindfulness" and "collective enactment." They studied various organizations—initially, an aircraft carrier, air traffic control, and electrical power generation—to learn how individuals within these systems coped during a catastrophe. And they asked, "How can companies make sure that disasters don't occur?" They eventually expanded their inquiry to include organizations from many sectors, such as commercial aviation, emergency rooms, firefighting units, and station houses.

One year later, in 2001, Weick and Sutcliffe published their landmark book, *Managing the Unexpected.* In that work, they codified their now-famous five principles of high reliability. The solid, evidence-based principles they offered appealed to a broad swath of healthcare leaders, who immediately sought to apply the principles to the unique challenges of their own industry.

The Five Principles

Weick and Sutcliffe researched organizations that effectively managed unforeseen setbacks, leading them to identify five key characteristics that tend to sustain positive organizational performance. Let's consider briefly each of the five:

1. *Preoccupation with Failure*

   HROs must pay continuous attention to anomalies that could indicate the presence of bigger problems in a system. Preoccupation with failure is about staying alert to small discrepancies and worrisome signs.

2. *Reluctance to Simplify*

   This principle cautions leaders to avoid the temptation of trying to make a complex situation appear simpler than it is. Oversimplifying a problem can often lead to overlooking the true or root causes of a troubling condition.

3. *Sensitivity to Operations*

   This principle is about seeing what individuals are *actually* doing in an organization, regardless of their intentions, plans, or stated strategies. *How* exactly are they operating? Are they doing *X* when they intended to do *Y*?

4. *Commitment to Resilience*

   This principle, when consistently applied, enables organizations to develop the ability to detect, contain, and bounce back from the inevitable errors that otherwise could disable the group. According to Weick and Sutcliffe, HROs "pay close attention to their capability to investigate, learn, and act *without* knowing in advance what they will be called to act upon."[17]

5. *Deference to Expertise*

   Workers at every level in an organization develop certain areas of know-how that others in the company don't possess. Leaders and employees in HROs habitually defer to those individuals who have the most expertise in any given situation, regardless of that individual's rank.

After the tremendous success of their book, Weick and Sutcliffe soon published two more bestsellers, which further expanded on the theme of managing the unexpected. The third edition of their first book was released in 2015 and continues to exert a profound influence on healthcare in the United States.

HRO Proponents and Agencies

The federal government's **Agency for Healthcare Research and Quality** released a 131-page guidebook for healthcare leaders in 2008. The document discusses how to use high reliability to improve patient care, and how to think about and change quality and safety in healthcare.

Using illustrations and attention-grabbing headlines, the AHRQ document highlights its key concepts, which are essentially the five principles of high reliability, but advice within the document tends to be broad and somewhat vague.

The document's recommendations essentially come down to making the public increasingly aware of medical errors and improving the quality of health information technology, such as electronic medical records, along with using Lean Six Sigma, a management approach that combines the waste-reducing, efficiency-improving focus of Lean manufacturing (introduced by Toyota in the 1950s) with the error-reducing, quality-improving focus of Six Sigma (Motorola's process of the 1980s).[18]

The resource typifies the thinking of many healthcare leaders who regularly study the theory of high reliability but lack the practical experience to make it a reality in healthcare.

The Joint Commission (TJC) accredits approximately 3,800 hospitals in the US—accounting for nearly 80 percent of all the nation's hospitals and 85 percent of its accredited hospitals.[19] TJC is made up of the American Hospital Association, the American Medical Association, the American Nurses Association, and many other academic and professional healthcare organizations.

TJC's mission is "to continuously improve health care for the public, in collaboration with other stakeholders, by evaluating health care organizations and inspiring them to excel in providing safe and effective care of the highest quality and value. [TJC does] this by setting quality standards, evaluating an organization's performance, and providing an interactive educative experience that provides innovative solutions and resources to support continuous improvement."[20]

We don't wish to downplay the efforts of The Joint Commission Center for Transforming Healthcare (JCCTH), yet since its creation in 2009, we've seen no objective evidence that those efforts have yielded a significant impact on healthcare.

About six hundred other US hospitals are accredited through **DNV Healthcare and its NIAHO specialty program** certification in high reliability.[21] With its world headquarters in Oslo, Norway, DNV has been in business since 1864, aiming to "safeguard life, property, and the environment."[22] Specializing in assurance and risk management, it is active in six business sectors: maritime, energy systems, digital solutions, supply chain and product assurance, business assurance, and The Accelerator, DNV's "new business area fueling exponential growth."[23] Its business assurance division provides certification in healthcare, one of four industries in which it does so. The five principles reign there, too.

Johns Hopkins and its **Armstrong Institute for Patient Safety and Quality** offers a Patient Safety and Quality Leadership Academy that follows the five principles and relies on Lean Six Sigma. There's also an independent **Patient Safety Coaches Academy** that offers training for "harm-free healthcare" and teaches the skills outlined in Charles A. Mowll's book, *Five Disciplines for Zero Patient Harm*.[24]

If you Google "high reliability healthcare," you will find hundreds of organizations, institutes, consultants, and other authorities pop up on your screen. The vast majority of them depend for their expertise, to one degree or another, on the five principles of Weick and Sutcliffe.

With so many entities in agreement, you might wonder if anyone has doubts about this approach. At least one highly qualified voice does.

A Dissenting Voice

One prominent national and international leader in patient safety today is a physician named Alan Frankel, a cardiac anesthesiologist. He has worked at Beth Israel Deaconess Medical Center and Brigham and Women's Hospital and in the past thirty years has assessed more than a thousand organizations and trained and certified more than three thousand healthcare leaders and managers in safety and reliability.[25]

He also founded his own private company, Safe & Reliable Healthcare (recently acquired by Vizient, a big consultant in the healthcare world). The material Frankel developed for Safe & Reliable Healthcare is his own intellectual property and provided the basis for his three books and many peer-reviewed publications.

Both of us know Dr. Frankel personally; in fact, he wrote the foreword for Jeff's 2021 book, *Transformative Healthcare: A Physician-Led Prescription to Save Thousands of Lives and Millions of Dollars.* In a thirty-page white paper of his own approach to high reliability healthcare, Dr. Frankel departs from the five principles of high reliability as framed by Weick and Sutcliffe.[26]

He prefers to place patient care firmly at the center of his system, which features four large domains: leadership, culture, knowledge, and learning systems. Under those four domains, he assigns several sub-domains.

Neither Dr. Frankel nor we imply that the five principles are deficient or faulty somehow. In fact, they're based on excellent research and have been profitably applied in many industries for more than two decades. We'll discuss in the next chapter why we think they aren't working in healthcare, but for now, we want to be clear that we believe Weick and Sutcliff's work is compelling and important.

Likewise, we both affirm that healthcare systems and hospitals can profitably adopt Dr. Frankel's framework to organize the curriculum of their patient safety academy, or at least some of their safety teaching. In our view, however, Dr. Frankel doesn't go far enough. He stops at defining the components of his framework without giving practical examples of them. And without specifics on how to put the structure to use, it's unlikely caregivers will bother incorporating it into their daily practice.

Even so, as an overall framework, it provides a useful way to think about safety. The point here is that Dr. Frankel calls his approach high reliability healthcare—and it does *not* echo the five principles.

Still, despite Dr. Frankel's less-than-enthusiastic embrace of the five principles as the foundation for high reliability healthcare, the widespread endorsement of the principles from the industry as a whole *should* have resulted in clear strides forward in the last twenty years. Unfortunately, that is not the case.

How Much Progress?

To Err Is Human reported back in 1999 that as many as 98,000 people died in any given year from medical errors occurring in hospitals.[27]

A 2016 report from Johns Hopkins University claimed that medical errors then accounted for about 250,000 deaths per year in the US, making it the third largest cause of death, above the 150,000 deaths caused by respiratory disease.[28]

To Err Is Human declared that legitimate liability concerns discouraged the reporting of errors.

Has much changed there? Not really.

In 2001, *Crossing the Quality Chasm* urgently called for a sweeping redesign of the American healthcare system.

That didn't happen.

The study also called for a 50 percent reduction in errors over the following five years.

That didn't happen, either.

An article by Dr. Carlos A. Pellegrini titled "Revisiting *To Err Is Human* 20 Years Later" indicates that although the 1999 report "and others have led to improvement in the healthcare system, the rates of familiar quality issues remain too high."[29]

Pellegrini also quotes Dr. Mark Chassin of The Joint Commission, who wrote, "We cannot continue to use the same methods and expect different results."[30]

With so much enthusiasm for building HROs, why have we made so little progress? Why hasn't our reliance on the five principles made a bigger difference? Why haven't the principles worked?

The Problem with "The Cure"

Dr. Chassin was right to say that we cannot continue to use the same methods and expect different results. Doing so is what Albert Einstein famously termed "insanity."

We've been driving down this same road for so many years, and mistakes in healthcare continue to be the third leading cause of death. It's obvious our current route will never take us where we want to go. Why?

For one, the healthcare system is driven by productivity, even though our service standard is often some form of "safety first." In practice, productivity—and not safety—becomes our priority. The bottom line takes precedence. We give bonuses for productivity, depending on how well an individual does on clinical scores. But while we advocate for safety scores, are we accountable for how safely we run a department or a hospital?

Why do we keep on trying to do the same thing over and over again while expecting different results? Multiple initiatives have been tried, none of which have worked.

It took disasters to change the way that the airline, nuclear power, and energy industries operate on a day-to-day basis. What will it take to motivate us in healthcare to move toward a new culture?

The Problem Is Bad Systems

When a 747 crashes, it tends to make headlines around the world. In healthcare, we have the equivalent of a 747 crash every day in the US, but so far, those tragedies have not become catalyzing events. Are we just not paying attention? Is there a Three Mile Island catastrophe in healthcare's future?

We believe that *To Err Is Human* was exactly right when it said that "the problem is not bad people in health care—it is that good people are working in bad systems that need to be made safer."[31] A major problem with healthcare's safety initiatives is that they are built upon an academic framework that's proven to be impractical for general use.

2

WHAT HASN'T WORKED

Hospitals spend millions of dollars every year on consultants, hoping to learn the secret to truly becoming an HRO. However, many consultants sell their standardized program regardless of the needs of the organization. To a hammer, everything is a nail. Additionally, most consultants fall back on the five principles of high reliability. They often rename and repackage them, but they're the principles, nonetheless.

We know a consultant who introduces the five principles under his own headings of culture and leadership and calls it his management system. Scores of people attend his $1,000-per-day seminars. As he presents the five principles, audience members smile, nod their heads appreciatively, and agree that being an HRO would feel great. But almost nothing they hear at his seminar changes *anything* back at their organizations.

Over the years, we've had experience with many such experts who are highly paid and "internationally recognized," yet offer the same fare and lackluster results.

Many of these consultants have never spent one day working as a healthcare professional and are unable to translate their experience effectively. Because of this, we've lost faith in the idea that consultants and seminars will lead to tangible improvements in reliability.

Why Have We Fallen So Short?

It's one thing to complain about a lack of progress. It's quite another to suggest why our efforts at achieving high reliability healthcare have fallen so short of our hopes and expectations.

Why do we think the five principles have failed to help us deliver significantly safer and more reliable healthcare? We believe three primary issues are to blame:

1. *The Five Principles Are Too Complicated*

   Written by a social psychologist and PhD management expert and issued by an academic publisher, *Managing the Unexpected* is full of dense, complex verbiage. Under the principle "Reluctance to Simplify," for instance, the authors make the following statement: "Organizing for more process variety means to increase your repertoire of actions that register and control variations in input."[32] It's not a user-friendly insight, is it? Another example is their explanation of a "Commitment to Resilience": "The juxtaposition of improvisation and resilience makes sense in the context of Ron Westrum's earlier argument that 'A system's willingness to become aware of problems is associated with its ability to act on them.'"[33]

   It takes time and effort to decipher the meaning of these wordy descriptions. While some may appreciate academic theories that require reflection and contemplation, they're not particularly helpful to a busy caregiver at a patient's bedside.

   Experts don't even agree on what the five principles mean.

   Clearly, we need something simpler. These ideas designed to help providers improve safety and reliability must be easy to understand.

2. *The Five Principles Address the Wrong Audience*

   In current healthcare practice, the five principles focus on *organizational concerns* rather than on *operational processes*. That means they're aimed at management, not at practitioners.

In line with this problem, we note a study that systematically reviewed articles investigating the use of Lean Six Sigma in healthcare. It found that far fewer studies focused on improving medical processes than they did on management processes.[34]

In practical terms, this suggests that no matter how much healthcare leaders study the concepts of high reliability, those concepts are not being applied at the right level and are not benefiting patient care.

Why, then, should we expect any results other than minimal movement toward high reliability healthcare?

3. *The Five Principles Don't Embed Themselves into the Culture*

   No initiative to make healthcare safer and more reliable will work unless whatever helpful changes that get made also get embedded into an organization's culture.

In a November 2019 editorial that appeared in *Modern Healthcare,* Dr. Mark Chassin—who served as a member of the committee that wrote *To Err Is Human*—declared that the US healthcare system still needs a drastic overhaul of its institutional culture.[35] That same month, on a podcast sponsored by the American Hospital Association, Chassin reflected on the significant lack of progress made in healthcare safety since the release of *To Err Is Human* twenty years before. He asked, "Who is satisfied with the current state?" and then added, "If we're not satisfied, we need to change the way we have been going about improvement."[36]

We couldn't agree more. The question is, *what* should we change and *how* should we change it?

Fortunately, a system already exists in a very different arena that has proven massively effective over the past seventy-five years. Those who created this system faced daunting challenges eerily similar to those we face in healthcare, and yet managed to turn around their ship, so to speak, so that today it boasts a safety and reliability record that is the envy of leaders around the world.

We'll get to the beginnings of that story in the next chapter, and in Part Two we'll focus more deeply on it. But for now, we'd like to introduce an extended metaphor that might help us all to understand why healthcare has latched onto an approach that, for more than twenty years, simply has not worked.

The Lesson of the Leeches

If the five principles of high reliability have not noticeably improved healthcare safety in more than two decades of trying, then why do hospitals, clinics, and other healthcare organizations still use them? If they haven't proven effective in widely generating high reliability healthcare, then why hasn't something else taken their place?

Maybe we can learn a lesson or two from the lowly leech.

For centuries, it was believed that leeches could be used to suck out "bad blood" in sick individuals, aiding in their cure. The earliest evidence we have of the practice comes from a mural in an Egyptian tomb dating from about 1500 BCE, in which an ancient physician was depicted using leeches to treat a patient.[37] Medical texts from ancient Greece and early Islamic physicians also expounded the theory and practice of using leeches to fight human ailments. The practice continued in one form or another until the late eighteenth century, when "a craze for leeching gripped Europe and North America and led to the collection, trade, and use of millions of leeches each year."[38]

While bloodletting was thought to balance the four "humors" of the body—blood, phlegm, black bile, and yellow bile—not until the late 1700s did it start to become the suggested remedy for a huge assortment of medical troubles, from headaches and fever to hemorrhoids and toothaches. A French doctor, François-Joseph-Victor Broussais, believed that inflammation caused all human illness and that bloodletting could decrease inflammation. He served as the chief physician at the Val-de-Grâce military hospital in Paris and treated all his patients with leeches, regardless of their diagnoses. Before him, no one had ever dealt with wounded soldiers and the very ill with such a treatment. But his approach soon caught on and "the leech craze spread quickly and soon transcended the borders of Paris and France," creating a "lucrative transnational industry" that provided "income for leech collectors and farmers, importers and exporters, apothecaries, quacks, and hucksters."[39]

Fascination with leeches rapidly spread to the general culture. Women wore dresses embroidered with leech patterns, poets waxed eloquent about the blood-sucking little beasts, and jars decorated with leech motifs graced apothecary shops and the homes of the wealthy. The craze was driven by societal economics, not medical efficacy.

At the height of the trend, France imported thirty-three *million* leeches in just one year. As the eighteenth century wound down, the widespread harvesting of medicinal leeches had resulted in their near extinction in England, Wales, Ireland, and the Netherlands. "In response," writes Martucci, "countries began farming leeches and importing wild ones from places as far away as Russia, Hungary, and the Ottoman Empire."[40]

Entrepreneurs redoubled their efforts to collect leeches, even creating large leech farms to meet demand. Poor conditions on many of these farms did little more than create disease and attract predators.

Two primary issues eventually conspired to bring an end to leech mania. First, various cholera outbreaks in the 1830s in Europe and North America dampened belief in the efficacy of bloodletting, since the use of leeches peaked in these years yet the plagues continued. As Martucci noted, "Leeches proved no match for the deadly cholera, and in the aftermath, leech therapy began a long decline."[41]

Second, germ theory began to overtake the four humors theory, prompting doctors around the world to look upon bloodletting with increasing suspicion. By the early twentieth century, bloodletting and leeches were both almost universally regarded as an unfortunate medical myth of the past.

And yet . . . that was not quite the end for modern medicine's use of the leech.

Starting in the 1970s, surgeons began to use leeches in microsurgery procedures to relieve venous congestion[42]. In 1985, the practice gained momentum when a surgeon used leeches to successfully reattach a severed ear to a young patient.[43] The case received wide publicity—it marked only the second time such an operation had succeeded—and leeches got a new lease on medical life, if vastly reduced in extent. In 2004, the FDA approved the medicinal use of leeches in reconstructive and plastic surgery, categorizing them as living, breathing medical devices.[44] Since that time, some physicians have begun to prescribe leeches for conditions as varied as varicose veins, neuropathy, blocked arteries, and osteoarthritis.

As a result, leech farming has made a bit of a comeback, although on a vastly smaller scale than in the nineteenth century. Biopharm, an international company based in South Wales, created "the first leech farm of its kind" as "innovators in the cultivation of the medicinal leech, currently producing the majority of leeches used in modern medicine worldwide," according to the company's website.[45]

Some might respond to all of this by saying, "Okay, that sounds interesting, but . . . *so what?* What do leeches have to do with high reliability healthcare?"

We see several disquieting parallels between the eighteenth-century fascination with medicinal leeches and the twenty-first-century reliance on the five principles of high reliability. Consider four key similarities:

1. Both leeches and the principles were originally used for very specific applications, but in time came to be applied—ineffectively—for broader uses unsuited to their natures.
2. Enormous, self-perpetuating industries grew up around both leeches and the principles, industries that did little to help patients or improve the practice of medicine.
3. Both were shown to be ineffective for their use, and there were better theories available in each case. Cholera outbreaks and the rise of germ theory brought an end to the leech craze. We hope that it will not take a catastrophe for modern medicine to recognize that

the principles have not worked. And we strongly believe that an alternate theory, already proven in another arena, will bring rapid improvement to healthcare reliability and thus greatly increase patient safety.

4. Neither leeches nor the principles are useless, but both can and have been used in ways that simply *cannot produce helpful or effective results*. Used in their proper spheres, however, both can perform extremely worthwhile functions.

How long did it take medical science to learn that the practice of using leeches not only didn't work, but also actively prevented doctors from finding approaches that actually *did* work?

Consider the case of the first president of the United States, George Washington. One day, at age sixty-seven, he began to feel the scratchiness and pain of a sore throat. The next day, he could barely speak and found it impossible to swallow a concoction of molasses, vinegar, and butter. His wife, Martha, summoned multiple doctors. Before the physicians arrived, Washington asked the plantation overseer to bleed him. The man did and stopped only when Martha thought he'd bled her husband too much.

The first doctor to reach Washington's home bled the former president again, and then again. Two more physicians arrived early that afternoon. The younger of the two declared that more bleeding would serve only to weaken Washington when he desperately needed his strength. The two older doctors ignored his counsel and bled the president yet again. They also induced vomiting, driven by the idea, common at the time, that whatever disease Washington had would then have "nothing left on which to work."[46]

By late afternoon, Washington felt the end coming. Somehow, he worked up the strength to get his affairs in order. He died just before midnight on December 14, 1799.

Afterward, one of the two older doctors confessed that if he and his colleague had "taken no more blood from [Washington], our good friend might have been alive now."[47] They still didn't know what ailment had afflicted the former president, but clearly their treatment did nothing to help.

While we don't believe the five principles are directly harming healthcare in the same way bleeding led to Washington's death, they are comparable in that the belief of their efficacy has kept practitioners from moving on to truly beneficial practices.

So then, *why are we still using leeches?*

No One Could Do a Better Job

A former boss of Bob's used to say about subordinates who consistently employed poor work habits, "No one could do a better job." While at first hearing it sounded like a compliment, he really meant that the job would be done better if no one did it at all. This is because it is better to *know* that no one is doing a job than it is to think that someone *is* doing it and to rely on them when in fact, they aren't.

"No one could do a better job" brings to mind an entertainment example. On an episode of *The Big Bang Theory*, one character, Amy Farrah Fowler, points out to her genius boyfriend, Sheldon Cooper, the problem in the movie *Raiders of the Lost Ark*.

"Indiana Jones plays no role in the outcome of the story," Amy explains. "If he weren't in the film, it would turn out exactly the same . . . The Nazis would have still found the ark, taken it to the island, opened it up, and all died. Just like they did."

Sheldon's jaw drops—literally. Amy is right, of course. Indy was superfluous. Though Sheldon claims to have watched the film thirty-six times, he had never realized how unnecessary his hero was. To be honest, neither had we! Is championing the five principles the same as rooting for our favorite movie character despite their lack of impact? Instead of believing that the job is getting done, would we be better off knowing that it's not? We become frustrated when we encounter self-proclaimed high-reliability experts who teach Weick and Sutcliffe's principles of high reliability without delving into more comprehensive, practical applications. Of such individuals it can honestly be said, "No one could do a better job."

3

MOVING BEYOND THE BOARDROOM

Practically everyone in US healthcare seems to agree that we need to change if our industry is to become as safe and reliable as it needs to be. Hope bloomed in many hearts when Weick and Sutcliffe arrived on the scene. Executives from across the healthcare spectrum immediately embraced the five principles of *Managing the Unexpected* and began the work of implementing those principles into their organizations. Nearly everyone wanted their group to become recognized as an HRO. Leaders from all over the US soon began attending seminars and taking coursework to get certified. They all hoped and expected that integrating the five principles into their workplaces would radically improve their safety and reliability performance.

Unfortunately, it didn't.

And yet, almost every day, we hear people from various institutions say, "We're on our journey to becoming a high reliability organization." If we ask them, "What do you mean by that?" they nearly always reply, "We have a commitment to safety. We have robust reporting. We use IT to catch mistakes."

We applaud every one of those initiatives. They're all excellent activities—but none of them create a high reliability organization. To create a true HRO, we have no choice but to change the culture, and the only way to change the culture is by focusing on individual behavior.

These days, many of us have begun to realize that the core challenge lies in transforming our culture. And not just culture in the boardroom, but culture in the organization at large, the kind of culture that boasts the power to reshape behavior at the ground level, on the front lines.

Why Have the Five Principles Remained in the Boardroom?

While we've already considered a few reasons why the five principles have not helped us achieve the kind of results we all desire, we'd like to go just a bit deeper.

Let's start by grasping that the five principles are formally grouped into two categories. Three of the principles are slotted under an "anticipation" category because they are crafted to help stop undesirable events from occurring. The three principles in this category include a *preoccupation with failure*, *reluctance to simplify*, and *sensitivity to operations*. All three principles are addressed to an organization as a whole and say, "If we focus here, we won't suffer those undesirable events."

Think of the boardroom of Southwest Airlines. These airline executives ask themselves, "How can we prevent a midair collision? How can we prevent a ground collision? How can we prevent catastrophic events due to adverse weather conditions?" They are rightly preoccupied with catastrophes because they know the financial and reputational costs such a disaster will have, to say nothing of the greatest cost—loss of human life. By anticipating issues correctly, leaders hope to save their companies from a world of hurt.

The second category is "containment," concerned with mitigating the consequences of a catastrophe after it happens. It also looks for ways to make sure a similar event doesn't happen again. The two principles in this category are *commitment to resilience* and *deference to expertise*. Again, they focus on the behavior of an organization and on the systems that can help it avoid the negative results it fears. None of these principles concern themselves with operations at an individual level.

If a passenger airliner goes down or a person dies at a theme park, everything comes to a screeching halt. Unfortunately, in many healthcare organizations, the permanent disablement or death of a patient gets less attention. In part, this is due to the nature of the industry—not all injuries can be healed, or diseases cured. But tragically, patients are sometimes seriously harmed or even killed by a clinician's error that could have been prevented.

In such cases, some healthcare organizations will try to hide the mistake from the family. If it can't be hidden, the hospital will work to keep the incident out of the public eye by paying the individuals involved and having them sign a non-disclosure agreement, as did VUMC in the Vaught incident. Hospitals will often do everything possible to keep the event from reaching the courts.

This lack of transparency grows from a fear of lawsuits and loss of business. It's understandable, but not helpful at resolving future problems. Fear can sometimes shift an organization's focus from patient safety to liability management.

Due to the nature of their roles and daily interactions with patients, frontline workers are the best-positioned people within a healthcare organization to champion a patient-safety focus and ensure positive, error-free outcomes.

This is why we need a different approach to high reliability, one that improves individual behavior throughout an organization.

Lessons from the Nuclear Navy

Weick and Sutcliffe investigated several industries as they prepared to write their book. They especially looked at commercial aviation and aircraft carrier flight operations but never considered the daily operations of the carrier's nuclear reactor. They investigated firefighting units and emergency rooms, but they considered the function of the latter units more than the individual care provided there by doctors and nurses. The emergency room study, in fact, focused on effective staging for specialty locations such as the trauma room and the heart room. It emphasized the optimal positioning of critical machines, equipment, and supplies. It did not focus on individual behavior or practice.

Perhaps Weick and Sutcliffe did not study the nuclear navy because it had never suffered a catastrophic reactor accident in all its years of operation. If you're writing a book on managing the unexpected, you might research industries that *had* suffered catastrophes but had afterward learned some valuable lessons about how to avoid future ones. It would also make sense to investigate what these groups did to mitigate the worst effects of the catastrophes even as they found themselves in the middle of them. If Weick and Sutcliffe *had* looked into the operations of the nuclear navy, they would have made some extraordinary discoveries.

For one thing, they would have learned that watchstanding principles had been developed to directly address and change traditional military culture that demanded of its sailors, "Do what you're told, don't challenge superiors, follow orders, don't ask questions." The watchstanding principles were designed to work on the individual level—something like a creed to live by—not the organizational level. They were meant to directly change behavior and practices on the ground (and on the sea).

Second, they would have seen how effectively the watchstanding principles worked to prevent reactor mishaps. (And keep in mind that the nuclear navy trains twenty-year-olds to operate these highly enriched nuclear power plants with the same fuel—uranium 235—used at Chernobyl, Three Mile Island, and Fukushima.)

Our crossover careers in the nuclear navy, healthcare, and safety and quality have uniquely positioned us to understand the benefits of the nuclear navy's watchstanding principles and its culture of high reliability, and to fit them to the needs of healthcare. Working together, we adapted the watchstanding principles into the five pillars of high reliability and put them to use throughout many hospitals, including the largest hospital in America.

If the culture of healthcare is to change significantly, we are convinced the five pillars must be ingrained in every individual who interacts with patients, just as they are ingrained in everyone in the nuclear navy. They must become a set of beliefs—a creed—that guides all individual actions. While we'll look more deeply into what this means in Part Two, at its root it means five key things. Allow us to give you a snapshot.

First, *every* healthcare worker must have a higher level of understanding. Second, *every* healthcare worker must have the integrity to do the right thing, whether anyone's looking or not. Third, there must be formality in their communication as well as in their procedures. Fourth, all must exhibit a questioning attitude. And fifth, workers must back each other up.

This is what high reliability healthcare is. Mastering academic theory at a managerial level will not be what transforms healthcare. If transformation is to happen anywhere, it must happen on the front line, through changed individual behavior at a patient's bedside.

And that will require integrating the five pillars into US healthcare.

We Must Put the Right Words into Action

The five pillars, unlike the five principles, give frontline personnel the right and most effective words to address errors and deficiencies. It would help nothing at all to say to a nurse, "You made that mistake. You know, your mistake falls under sensitivity to operations. Why didn't you have sensitivity to operations?"

What a difference once the five pillars get put to work on the front line! In that case, someone might say instead, "Why didn't you speak up when you noticed that error?" or "Can you tell me why you didn't have a questioning attitude the moment you sensed something didn't feel quite right?"

If we want to change the culture, we must attach simple, memorable words to the actions of our colleagues instead of trying to use academic or theoretical terms. When someone makes an error, it's critically important to focus on expected behavior, not to place blame, but so that correct, appropriate, or safe behavior becomes the norm.

Leaders have struggled to operationalize the current high reliability principles. At an organizational level, they can be useful in the right context and provide a conceptual framework for avoiding catastrophes and recovering from them. But we must not forget that they're theoretical. They're academic. They were never meant to morph into practical application, as we mentioned in the last chapter. The principles were not intended to be stated in a way that elicits effective individual behavior.

The five principles are talked about at safety seminars, high reliability events hosted by national organizations, and in board rooms, but because they are so difficult to operationalize, they are rarely, if ever, mentioned at the clinical level. Indeed, many caregivers would be hard-pressed to name even one of the principles. The principles therefore have no power to change the behavior of those providing care on the ground. And so, regardless of how much the principles might get discussed at higher levels in the organization, the culture shifts hardly at all.

The five pillars, on the other hand, go straight to individual behavior. They continually ask, "What is that doctor or nurse who's providing the care actually *doing*?"

Picking the Right Tools

It's important to recognize that both the principles and the five pillars are just tools. Like all tools, they're made for very specific and yet different purposes. The principles and the pillars are not interchangeable, as if they were both scalpels produced by separate manufacturers. They're useful for very different things, as though one were a heart monitor and the other a clamp.

The principles are designed to be employed on a high organizational level, specifically to anticipate or halt the development of catastrophes. They also can be used to guide the actions of an organization after a disaster strikes. Their design is specific to those two unique conditions.

Weick and Sutcliffe's audience was not frontline personnel. They never said, "If you teach these principles to every doctor and nurse, you'll have a high reliability organization." We believe that Weick and Sutcliffe never intended for their book to serve as a guide for the daily operations of healthcare. But due to the absence of any other guide or dependable process, that's exactly how it came to be used. Healthcare workers must have both theoretical knowledge *and* practical application. Although we have tools that can enable practitioners to gain both, we lack an overall, concrete training plan for *how* to do it. Fortunately for us, the nuclear navy already has shown us how.

The five pillars give us a powerful tool for day-to-day use by all healthcare workers. The five pillars are framed in easy-to-understand language and focus on *how* individuals are doing their jobs, regardless of what those jobs might be. In other words, the five pillars put a spotlight on behavior.

Time for a Reset

We all agree that healthcare culture needs to change. But to change our culture, we must change individual behavior on the ground. While the five principles have shown no ability to change individual behavior, especially on the front line, the five pillars were designed to do *exactly* that.

People, not organizations or management systems, are the ones who get things done in healthcare. We must therefore place our focus firmly on individual human beings.

Genuine high reliability healthcare will grace our institutions when every doctor, nurse, tech, and aide has a voice; when colleagues are an integral part of a team that cares about them; when they have a higher level of understanding about their specific tasks; when they carry with them a questioning attitude and are people of integrity; when they frame key communications in formal ways to avoid misunderstanding and follow formal procedures; and when they habitually back each other up.

That's the formula the nuclear navy used to build itself into the world's leading HRO, and that's how we can do the same in healthcare.

What Have We Got to Lose?

We have no need to spend more time and money trying, yet again, to adapt the five principles for healthcare. They've had more than enough opportunity to prove their effectiveness at changing our culture, yet they haven't.

Fortunately, we have an alternative. In fact, at many hospitals, we've already begun to adapt and utilize the five pillars from the nuclear navy—an approach that has more than proven itself through two extremely difficult accomplishments:

1. Vastly improving a huge organization's safety and reliability record
2. Permanently reshaping a whole organizational culture to work hand in glove with enhanced safety protocols

The US Navy has employed its watchstanding principles for seventy-five years and has achieved an unparalleled record of safety within the nuclear industry. We believe the five pillars have the power to radically reshape safety and reliability in healthcare as well.

What do we have to lose?

PART TWO

NUCLEAR SOLUTIONS

4

RICKOVER'S DILEMMA

Hyman G. Rickover had a problem.

Shortly after World War II and decades before people started calling him "the father of the nuclear navy," Rickover had the idea of powering US submarines with nuclear reactors. While the concept made perfect sense to him, most of his immediate superiors in the navy scoffed at the idea. And it didn't help his cause that many of them also intensely disliked him.

And yet, Rickover prevailed over opposition to his vision, antagonism toward his person, and resistance to a new kind of military culture that had to come into existence if his vision were to succeed.

How did he do it? This isn't just an interesting historical question for us, because we believe it has a direct bearing on what happens to the future of healthcare and our desire to equip high reliability organizations.

Back to the Beginning

Rickover started life as Chaim Gdala Rykower, born on January 27, 1900, to Jewish parents living in Poland (then Makov, Russia). The family fled the Russian Revolution of 1905 and landed in New York City, soon moving to Chicago, where he grew up as Hyman G. Rickover.[48]

He won an appointment to the US Naval Academy in 1918 (where he substituted "George" for his given middle name) and graduated in 1922,

107th out of 540 midshipmen. Commissioned as an ensign, he served first on a destroyer and then on the battleship *Nevada*. He earned a master's degree in electrical engineering from Columbia University in 1929 and applied for submarine service; they turned him down because he was considered too old. But as he left the building where he'd just been rejected, he bumped into his former commanding officer on the *Nevada*, who persuaded naval authorities to approve his request.[49]

He served on submarines from 1929 to 1933. In 1937, he commanded a minesweeper for three months, where he received a promotion to lieutenant commander. Soon afterward he landed at the Bureau of Engineering in Washington, DC. During World War II, he gained experience in directing several naval development programs—and earned significant notoriety.[50] *Time* magazine once featured Rickover in an article that described his wartime service like this:

> Sharp-tongued Hyman Rickover spurred his men to exhaustion, ripped through red tape, drove contractors into rages. He went on making enemies, but by the end of the war he had won the rank of captain. He had also won a reputation as a man who *gets things done*.[51]

After the US Army Air Corps dropped atomic bombs on Hiroshima and Nagasaki, bringing an abrupt end to the war, the navy decided it could harness atomic power to drive its destroyers. Rickover was directed to work with General Electric to design a nuclear-powered propulsion plant. He quickly became convinced that placing nuclear reactors on submarines should take precedence over destroyers. His immediate superiors disliked the idea. They soon reassigned him to "advisory duties" and gave him an office in an abandoned women's bathroom.[52]

Undeterred, Rickover and his staff skirted those superior officers and went straight to a fellow former submariner, Fleet Admiral Chester

Nimitz, then chief of naval operations. Nimitz endorsed Rickover's idea and took it to the secretary of the navy, John L. Sullivan, who later championed the idea.[53]

Why Build Nuclear Submarines?

Submersibles during World War II could operate underwater for only a limited number of hours. Their diesel engines needed both air and fuel to operate, and the submarines' batteries had to be recharged every couple of days. The subs couldn't get air while underwater, so to recharge their batteries, they had to surface. This made them extremely vulnerable to enemy radar and aircraft and led to one of the most sobering statistics of World War II: submariners had a one in five chance of not coming home, the highest fatality rate in the military.[54]

Rickover realized that a nuclear-powered submarine wouldn't have the same vulnerability. Without the need to recharge batteries, the missions of nuclear-powered submarines would be limited in length only by the food supply and physical needs of the crew. This could forever change national security.

Unfortunately, nuclear-powered subs would be massively more complicated to design and operate than conventional subs. Developers had countless complex barriers to overcome. How do you harness a vast energy source in such a small space? What coolant do you use? How do you protect sailors from radiation? How do you manage steam? (Until then, submarines did not use steam.) How would radiation from the nuclear reactor affect construction materials? Developers quickly created prototypes with scram abilities—a way to immediately and safely shut down a reactor in case of an emergency.

Rickover understood that he needed tight safeguards around all this new development. If he didn't have them, those in power would be quick to shut down everything he wanted to do.

Fear of the Bomb

The unleashed power of the atom in the 1950s led to a great worldwide fear of the bomb and of nuclear power in general. On December 8, 1953—just eight years after Hiroshima and Nagasaki—President Dwight D. Eisenhower gave his famous "Atoms for Peace" speech at the United Nations. "Who can doubt that, if the entire body of the world's scientists and engineers had adequate amounts of fissionable material with which to test and develop their ideas, [atomic energy] would rapidly be transformed into universal, efficient, and economic usage?"[55] he asked. To provide some answers to his question, he established the Atomic Energy Commission.

Rickover knew that in such a fear-of-the-bomb culture there would be zero tolerance for even one radiation leak on a submarine. A single mishap would surely kill the program. He was determined to keep that from happening.

As he supervised the design and construction of the very first nuclear submarine, someone asked him, "Can we reduce the shielding around the reactor? We can't afford the extra weight or the volume."

But Rickover wouldn't hear of it. "No sir, I'm going to use civilian standards throughout, the ones approved by the United Nations medical advisers [and] the World Health Organization . . . the civilian standards will be fully met. I don't want any corners cut."[56]

The Soviets, America's main adversaries at that period, built many more nuclear subs than the US did, and in much less time. They also had uncounted numbers of sailors die of leukemia; their leaders simply didn't care.[57] Their nuclear subs suffered *many* serious reactor mishaps, sometimes leading to the loss of those subs and their entire crews.

Rickover refused to put up with any of that. He demanded that both his engineers and the navy's contractors meet or exceed his extremely high specifications for putting reactors on submarines.

But he also knew that wouldn't be enough. He recognized that if he had in place even the best equipment and technology available, human error could still cause a disaster. But how could he minimize human error? He quickly realized that he needed to change the existing culture of the navy itself, which would be anything but easy.

How Do You Transform a Whole Culture?

Rickover recognized that his vision of nuclear-powered submarines would never work in the military culture of the 1950s, which had existed for generations. Soldiers, seamen, airmen, and Marines alike were told to:

> Follow orders!
>
> Do what you're told!
>
> Don't ask questions!
>
> Never contradict superiors!

The old command and control structure in place was both situational and hierarchical. You told the truth only if it made sense to. No sailor would tell his superior, "Sorry, but I failed to close a valve, and that's why we were in dry dock for two days." If he did, he might find himself in the brig or on KP duty for six months. No, you kept your mouth shut.

Rickover understood that such a culture could not possibly work in the new nuclear navy, where one reactor accident on a sub would mean the end of the whole program. The typical command-and-control structure based on hierarchy and situational ethics had to be replaced. But with what?

Rickover needed a new culture where everyone embraced their individual responsibility to speak up if they saw something out of place. He needed the kind of culture that celebrated the discovery of errors and took immediate steps to correct them. Such an alternative culture had to come from the very top and remain living and active in every sailor, at all times, regardless of rank.

Rickover built the culture he knew the nuclear navy needed on the foundation of his watchstanding principles. From the very beginning, he made the following demands of everyone in the program:

> I expect you to speak up.
>
> I expect you to have a higher level of understanding.
>
> I want you to challenge any procedure or operation that doesn't seem to make sense.
>
> I insist that you never act blindly like a robot.

But could he, in fact, create this new culture? Could he really replace the decades-old system with a very different one? Would this alternate culture infuse the whole organization, from top-level brass to the lowest-ranking sailor? Could *anyone* bring about such a massive but necessary change?

Rickover knew he could, but also knew it wouldn't be easy. He wrote, "Good ideas are not adopted automatically. They must be driven into practice with courageous impatience. Once implemented, they can be easily overturned or subverted through apathy or lack of follow-up, so a continuous effort is required."[58]

The First Nuclear Submarine

Rickover believed the grief he endured was worth it if it would give his country a potent new deterrent to war. He once said that it's better to sin against God than against bureaucracy, because God can forgive you.[59] Innumerable times, Rickover would come under fire for angering one or more of his superior officers.

Despite their dislike of Rickover and their initial resistance, the traditional military establishment finally agreed, albeit grudgingly, to support nuclear-powered submarines. However, they believed it would take at least twenty-five to forty years before the required technology could be developed.

Not quite. In early 1954, just three years after Congress authorized the construction of the first nuclear-powered submarine, the USS *Nautilus* was christened and launched. In the summer of 1958, the *Nautilus* left Pearl Harbor to cruise for the first time ever beneath the North Pole.[60]

Under the command of Captain William R. Anderson, the sub carried a crew of 116 men, including four civilian scientists. The boat maintained an average depth of about five hundred feet below the surface of the ice, but at one point came within five feet of it. By the time the *Nautilus* popped up in the North Atlantic on August 3, 1958, on its way to Iceland, it had become a global sensation.[61]

President Eisenhower presented Captain Anderson with a Legion of Merit award in a ceremony at the White House. Afterward, the captain made a special trip to see now–Rear Admiral Rickover, who'd been snubbed by many top navy brass who didn't want to give him any credit or publicity.

Rickover's greatest feat was not that he built the *Nautilus* in three years or that the sub sailed for a thousand miles under the polar ice cap; it was that he managed to change the navy culture so radically that it led to an unmatched legacy of safety.

But did Hyman G. Rickover pay a large personal price for his commitment? Indeed, he did—as will anyone who sets out to transform a long-established but underperforming culture.

The Price He Paid

Rickover's almost impossibly high standards made him very difficult to work for, but his co-workers loved him because he took pains to care for them.

For a long time, Rickover lacked the support he needed from the Department of Defense to build his nuclear navy. When Rickover was a captain and purposefully being passed over for admiral, he reached the point where he thought he would soon be out of the navy, but his co-workers had his back. Members of his staff met with senators and newspaper reporters on his behalf and leveraged their influence to fight for his promotion. They believed in his vision and felt convinced that the impact he would have on national security trumped everything else.

Many leaders care a lot about impressing those higher up the ladder than they, and very little about the folks on the rungs below. Rickover was just the opposite. He focused on his people and cared little about what the people above him thought; he cared even less about climbing ladders.

Rickover functioned as he did because he believed that everyone must look after their work just as conscientiously as if it were their own business and their own money. Temporary custodians would see the job only as a stepping stone to a higher position; they would never consider the long-term interests of the organization. A leader's lack of commitment to their present job would be perceived clearly by those under them, and they in turn would spend their entire working lives looking for the next job. By contrast, Rickover thought that when individuals valued their *present* job and acted accordingly, they'd have no reason to be concerned about their *next* job.

And that's exactly how he himself lived.

Rickover was anti-establishment and a non-conformist. Though many of his superiors in the US Navy and the Department of Defense dismissed him, he and his staff made the right connections with Congress, and people in power eventually listened to what he had to say.

Neither of us ever met Rickover (he became a four-star admiral in 1973, retired in 1982, and died in 1986), but we've heard many firsthand accounts of the notorious admiral and his exacting expectations.[62]

Jeff's friend Howard "Scotty" Flink, a navy petty officer first class who later transferred to the army and became a brigadier general, recounted an interview he'd had with Rickover much earlier in his naval career. Vying for a coveted spot on a nuclear submarine, Scotty, a petty officer at the time, arrived at the appointed interview room, where he found a handful of other interviewees already present and seated. The occupied chairs were sizeable and cushioned, but the sole vacant seat was a compact metal folding chair.

Scotty bent his large frame onto the cold chair, and soon after, Rickover entered the room and began the meeting.

Not only did Rickover notice the folding chair where Scotty sat without a fidget or complaint for the duration of the one-hour meeting, but Rickover had also placed the uncomfortable chair in the room beforehand as a sort of test. He wanted to see who had the humility to take it. The chair had been part of the interview.

Scotty got the submarine assignment.

Rickover's Legacy

A nuclear reactor accident, by definition, is the release into the environment of fissile material. It's remarkable that in over seven decades, the nuclear navy has never had such an accident among its more than 150 nuclear power plants on board its submarines, aircraft carriers, and cruisers.

Can you ever achieve such a record without the right culture, accountability, or high standards that everyone in the organization both knows and follows? Not a chance.

Had Hyman G. Rickover not put his watchstanding principles in place and, with them, changed the nuclear navy's culture, the navy surely would have suffered a Chernobyl or a Three Mile Island long ago.

Two Key Rickoids

Any lessons from the nuclear navy that we might want to highlight would start with two "Rickoids" (quotes from Admiral Rickover that have survived the test of time).

Here's the first: "What it takes to do a job will not be learned from management courses. It is principally a matter of experience, the proper attitude, and common sense, none of which can be taught in a classroom. Human experience shows that people, not organizations or management systems, get things done."[63]

Reading books and articles, going to conferences, and getting academic certifications in healthcare will not move the needle. What we need is a radical culture change that starts at the top and takes hold in very practical ways at every level in all healthcare organizations.

Here's the second Rickoid: "To practice a profession, one must have acquired mastery of an academic discipline, as well as technique for applying this special knowledge to the problems of everyday life. A profession is therefore intellectual in content, practical in application."[64]

We must marry academic rigor to practical application. Our people must *know*, and they must be able to *do*. Nothing less will suffice if healthcare is to become a high reliability industry.

Lessons for Healthcare

While it's clear Rickover's legacy has made a lasting impact on one of the highest-stakes organizations in the world, the similarities between the nuclear navy and the medical field may be less obvious. In fact, our focus here on a navy admiral may seem odd and out of place in a book purportedly about healthcare.

Consider, though, the don't-ask-questions culture of the navy at the time Rickover began his program. That same type of culture can still be found in healthcare among old-school practitioners who view any questions as affronts to their authority.

Just as sailors in the navy were hesitant to question a superior officer—especially a fierce, punishing one—until the principle of a questioning attitude was ingrained, nurses and techs will mostly keep quiet when faced with a dictatorial surgeon or department head.

This hierarchical culture is just one of many similarities between the nuclear navy and healthcare. In the next chapter, we'll examine more ways the two fields are alike.

Hyman G. Rickover saw how things were done in the navy and knew it was not good enough. He understood that he needed better guardrails than the ones then in existence. He simply couldn't afford a nuclear accident. With high expectations and consistency, he created a culture of transparency and accountability—a culture that led to unparalleled performance.

That same sense of urgency Rickover felt in the nuclear navy seventy years ago may still be lacking in healthcare. At a minimum, it's clear that we don't have the right guardrails in place.

As we'll see in the next chapter, the commonalities between the nuclear navy and healthcare are so compelling that it would be foolish to ignore the nuclear navy's journey and the keys to its success. And *that's* why we're talking about a navy admiral in a book about improving healthcare.

5

DRAWING COMPARISONS

It doesn't take the proverbial brain surgeon to see that submarines and hospitals are very different. For one thing, hospitals are not generally encased in metal and submerged in the icy waters of the Arctic. For another, no one on a submarine is slicing into an abdomen, repairing heart defects, or performing organ transplants.

In light of these differences, why do we imagine that it makes sense to take something like the watchstanding principles—designed for the nuclear navy to keep its submarines' reactors safe and working properly—and try to apply them to modern healthcare? How could such an idea have any possible merit?

Centuries ago, Tertullian, an early Christian author, wrote, "What has Jerusalem to do with Athens . . . ?" because he believed Christianity and classical Greek scholarship were so dissimilar that one could not possibly learn anything from the other.[65]

But Augustine, another Christian leader, took a more open-minded approach. Not only did Augustine answer Tertullian's question, but he also wrote an entire book in which he laid out the many areas Christianity could benefit from Greek scholars. This work, book IV of *Confessions,* influenced the very structure of the Christian church as it exists today.

We have no intention here of comparing ourselves with Augustine, and we're not qualified to speak about Athens and Jerusalem. But we *can* confidently declare that the nuclear navy clearly has much to offer contemporary healthcare. The two share many similarities as well as clear differences. Let's consider several of each and then focus on four key takeaways.

How Are They Alike?

First, both the nuclear navy and healthcare have significant variations in culture from one unit, department, or local organization to another. In both the navy and in healthcare, you can find units with great cultures led by caring individuals, and other units with struggling cultures led by iron-fisted autocrats. The side effect of the latter type of culture is a lack of psychological safety, which is needed for the questioning attitude essential in high-stakes fields.

Bob's first submarine post was on the USS *West Virginia* under the command of an authoritarian leader. Bob vividly remembers the menacing culture and the dangerous situations that arose because crew members were too afraid to speak up.

What Bob experienced on the *West Virginia* was similar to what many physicians experienced during their training as residents—yelling, demeaning comments, and other forms of punishment. Unfortunately, some physicians schooled in these toxic cultures perpetuate them with an attitude that says, "This is the way I learned, and if it worked for me, it should work for others."

Second, both navy recruits and healthcare workers sign up for a career of service. People who do so are generally caring individuals who want to make a positive difference in the world. Issues such as poor culture, lack of standards, accountability, transparency, and a general lack of support all combine to discourage staff and instill an attitude of apathy.

Safety issues on a nuclear-powered submarine and in the delicate work of medical professionals correlate directly with this apathy. Culture is nearly always at the root of every success and failure, whether in the nuclear navy or in healthcare.

Third, both the US Navy and American healthcare are very large.

It costs about $212 billion to operate the US Navy each year.[66] It has about 350,000 active-duty personnel, with another fifty-six thousand in the reserves.[67] The navy tallies about 251 active ships, including sixty-eight submarines.[68] That's *big*.

Americans spent $4.7 trillion on healthcare in 2023.[69] The US boasts more than six thousand hospitals that together offer over 916,000 beds.[70] About 227 healthcare systems operate up to five hospitals; seven systems operate more than one hundred hospitals; and 219 systems offer a thousand or fewer beds.[71] In 2022, the US counted more than a million doctors, almost four million nurses, and over seven million hospital employees. That's also big![72]

Fourth, healthcare and the navy share similar command structures. In the navy, the chain of command starts with the US president and moves to the vice president, the secretary of defense, the secretary of the navy, the chief of naval operations, and then on down the line to admirals, vice admirals, rear admirals, captains, commanders, lieutenant commanders, lieutenants, ensigns, and warrant officers.

A national healthcare system will have a board chair and president/CEO at the top, with various executive vice presidents, senior VPs, a chief clinical officer, executive directors, department heads, and so on throughout the organization, all of them in charge of various regions or functions.

Part of the reason why some navy systems can adapt so well to healthcare is because of their similar leadership structures.

Fifth, both the navy and healthcare operate units of various sizes, from the very large to the quite small. The largest aircraft carrier in the navy is the USS *Gerald R. Ford*, at 1,092 feet long, with a flight deck over six acres in size, carrying up to seventy-five aircraft, and a crew of about 4,600.[73] The largest hospital in America has over 2,245 beds.[74] The smallest ship in the navy is a security tugboat called a "Boomin Beaver," at nineteen feet long (the size of a Ford F-150), a draft of five feet, and a crew of two.[75] One of the smallest hospitals in America is Grace Cottage Hospital in Townshend, Vermont, with sixteen physicians and nineteen beds.[76]

As you can see, the US Navy and American healthcare have more in common than one might expect. And those commonalities may suggest that an approach used in one might be readily adaptable to the other.

How Do They Differ?

The first obvious difference between the nuclear navy and healthcare comes down to training. The training sailors receive in the nuclear navy is much more homogenous than the training of clinicians. There is one nuclear navy power school in the US, and all enlisted sailors and officers bound for a nuclear submarine must attend that school. While there, they learn Rickover's watchstanding principles. Everyone working on a submarine knows the standards of high reliability because everyone went through the same course. By contrast, healthcare workers are educated and trained by a multitude of programs and institutions. For example, there are approximately one thousand institutions in the US that offer an accredited BSN program.[77] There is no guarantee that caregivers completing their respective programs will be taught standards of high reliability.

Second, leaving a job in healthcare is much different than leaving a naval enlistment or commissioning. In healthcare, nobody will stop you if you want to go—you can simply quit. In the navy, you don't have that option. "Quitting" is tantamount to desertion and will land you in a great deal of trouble (and maybe in the brig).

Third, healthcare tends to focus on individual heroes—like the lead surgeon—whereas the navy focuses on the team. Sailors on nuclear submarines must work as a unit with their crewmates; they talk about what "they" accomplish, not what "I" accomplish.

Fourth, sailors in the nuclear navy know they must live with each other for months at a time, 24/7. The smaller the ship, the more likely they are to see and collaborate closely with one another for that whole period. In healthcare, workers may do twelve-hour shifts together, but then they go home. When a critically ill patient gets admitted in the middle of the night, the team on duty at the time is responsible for that patient's care—but only for the next several hours. Once a healthcare worker goes home, their responsibility for that patient comes to an end, and the temporary team of caregivers who were on duty together is disbanded.

Fifth, sailors can't visit their local union representative when they are unhappy at work. There are no unions in the navy. Not every hospital or care center works with unions, but many do, and all hospitals have human resources departments. If a hospital wants to change its culture, very often it must work closely with a union to make the changes it sees as necessary. If the union dislikes the proposed changes, the hospital may find it very difficult to change its culture. And all changes at every hospital must go through the HR department.

Sixth, the US Navy does not have to worry about civil lawsuits nearly as much as healthcare organizations do. While in specific situations, private citizens can bring a claim against a federal agency, a 1950 court case known as Feres v. United States went all the way to the Supreme Court, which determined that service members cannot file for damages under the Federal Tort Claims Act. Healthcare has no such legal protection.[78] The annual cost of medical malpractice suits comes to about $2.2 billion a year.[79]

The forward-thinking Augustine knew that some struggle and tension would occur when comparing Athens and Jerusalem. The same can be said of the nuclear navy and American healthcare. But from what we've already experienced, we know the lessons that can be learned from the navy, and we are confident of the benefits despite the differences.

6

LEADERSHIP AND CULTURE

The essential foundation for the nuclear navy and any other organization striving for high reliability is healthy leadership and culture. These elements serve both as an organization's bedrock and its most powerful tools. While it's possible to impose various standards, their effectiveness is limited if there isn't a culture that nurtures a genuine concern for team members. Attempting to implement programs or processes without fostering a caring culture can be futile. Unfortunately, many leaders fail to grasp this fundamental concept. They may profess to care, but they fail to follow through with actions.

Real evidence of concern should start with the highest leadership and flow through every level of an organization. When a company neglects to make the well-being of its team members a top priority, it cannot expect team members to care about the well-being of the company.

Good Tools, Bad Culture

Without the appropriate culture in place, even the finest tools on the planet will not operate as intended. Rickover's enduring influence, marked by transparency, accountability, and a commitment to watch-standing principles, remains evident on all submarines. The necessary tools exist, and the training received by all members of the nuclear navy reflects the high standards set by Rickover. Despite this, why do some nuclear submarines experience significant incidents, such as groundings, at-sea collisions, or a reduction in safety margins that could potentially lead to a nuclear accident?

While it is crucial to establish efficient procedures, incorporate redundancies, and define explicit expectations, it's essential to recognize that the lack of robust leadership and a nurturing organizational culture can still lead to the possibility of a catastrophic incident.

Bob's first commanding officer, the authoritarian captain of the *West Virginia*, stood about six foot six. He allowed his physical stature to enhance his rule through intimidation, filling his submarine with so much fear that his sailors stopped thinking critically. They felt paralyzed.

When Bob began his tour on the ship at age twenty-three, he learned of an incident that had taken place shortly before his arrival. A crew member on board the *West Virginia* had developed appendicitis and required an operation. Though the independent duty corpsman (medic) could perform certain emergency surgeries, conducting procedures on board a submarine was not a preferred solution.

Following protocol, the CO transmitted a message to fleet command describing the situation. The *West Virginia* was in the middle of the Atlantic Ocean, between the Azores and the East Coast. Awaiting the response to his message, he presumed the destination would be on the East Coast of the United States, so he headed the ship in that direction.

But when the answer from fleet command came in several hours later, the orders were to head to the Azores—the opposite direction. Unfortunately, the order came with many other messages, and while most of the crew was asleep. It went unnoticed for several more hours until the changing of the watch stander. Once the mistake was recognized and crew members realized they would have to tell the captain that they had gone six hours out of their way, fear gripped them. In fact, the crew seemed more worried about their CO's inevitable explosion than about the critical condition of their crew member. The sailors argued over who would tell the captain. When someone finally did, chaos ensued.

The CO started screaming, "All ahead flank, opposite direction!" The ship did an about-face to the Azores, maximum speed, its reactor operating at 100 percent—extremely close to thermal limits.

The *Trident* ballistic submarine was equipped with a pair of large lube oil coolers responsible for chilling its massive main engines. Under normal operating conditions, only one of these lube oil coolers was actively in use, while the other remained in standby mode. These coolers utilized seawater, passing it through a heat exchanger, to regulate the lube oil temperature.

On that particular day, the person in charge of overseeing the lube oil coolers noticed that the temperature of the lube oil leaving the active cooler exceeded the specified limit by one degree. Since the maximum seawater flow rate had already been achieved, the only available course of action to address this issue and prevent any potential criticism for recording an out-of-specification reading without taking corrective measures was to transition to the backup lube oil cooler. The standby cooler, being less frequently used, was expected to have a lower likelihood of marine growth buildup that could impair its performance.

The decision to switch between lube oil coolers, potentially interrupting the flow of lube oil, to an engine running at maximum rated speed for a mere one-degree temperature deviation may seem illogical. However, in the mind of the mechanic, avoiding criticism and the need to take corrective action prevailed, prompting the decision to make the switch.

He therefore reached out to maneuvering to seek approval for switching to the second cooler. In a maneuvering section, there is an engineering officer of the watch who directly supervises the throttle man, reactor operator, and electrical operator. Even though shifting the lube oil coolers while the ship was operating at full throttle seemed illogical, the engineering officer granted permission to proceed. None of the individuals in maneuvering raised any questions about this decision, and they didn't bother informing the watchstanding supervisor about the planned change. Their focus wasn't on the ship's safety but rather on finding ways to avoid the commanding officer's wrath.

The young man made the switch without following procedure. He was supposed to first open the lube oil vent to let out all the air, but he didn't. The instant the young mechanic shifted the lube oil coolers, an enormous pocket of air rushed into the main engine, causing a catastrophic failure to half of the main engines.

It proved to be an exceedingly expensive error. The submarine remained in port for a three-month period, undergoing extensive repairs, all due to a single sailor's incorrect adjustment of a valve. But was it really because of this one mistake?

As we dig into the five pillars of high reliability in the next chapter, it will become all too clear that the crew members in this story failed to uphold standards that had been ingrained in them. Most notably, they failed to question why a message was not promptly read and routed, which would have avoided the need for maximum speed, the critical thinking when shifting lube oil coolers, and the failure to back up the novice watch stander. The unhealthy culture on board the *West Virginia* overrode the crew member's training and led to extreme apathy. The sailors didn't do their jobs because they were afraid to.

The Difference Culture Makes

After the nightmare of serving on a ship with a tyrannical captain, Bob had the opportunity to serve under a polar-opposite leader, Bruce Grooms. The level of caring and openness to feedback that Captain Grooms exhibited surprised Bob at first. But he soon saw the excellent culture and results that such leadership would yield—results far superior to those of his former captain. From then on, Bob paid close attention to the culture-building and culture-destroying habits of the various leaders he encountered, and he grew more and more convinced that all successful organizations must be rooted in a healthy culture.

Bob's understanding of the critical importance of organizational culture grew when he assumed command of the USS *Texas*. His primary task was to certify the new *Virginia*-class submarine for arctic operations and transit to the North Pole. This challenge came about only three months into his new position as he led the underperforming crew he had inherited.

As Bob settled into his role, he realized that the significant recurring safety issues on the submarine were not solely due to the absence of clear processes or procedures. Instead, the root cause of these issues lay in the crew's perception that the command did not genuinely care for their well-being. This lack of care resulted in a lack of commitment from the crew to the ship's welfare and overall mission.

In order to change the attitude and performance of his team, Bob drew inspiration from his past experiences. He understood that effective leadership required prioritizing the well-being of the crew over other considerations, such as profit margins or personal career advancement. Misplaced priorities will ultimately lead to safety issues and hinder long-term success.

While Bob recognized the significance of the organization's mission, he knew that the well-being and morale of employees should always take precedence.

As crew members saw and felt the evidence of their new commander's priorities, the culture on board the ship improved rapidly—and with it, safety scores and performance. And the first-of-its-kind mission to the North Pole was completed successfully.

Not everyone has the example of a Bruce Grooms to learn from. Many leaders value the wrong things and don't connect the dots between a caring culture and a safe, successful organization. Without laying the right foundation, it's impossible to achieve lofty organizational goals.

For an illustration of this important point, let's step out of the naval and healthcare fields for a moment. Imagine, if you will, a restaurant that rarely gets recognized by food critics, often receives bad reviews for quality and service, and sometimes comes close to failing its health code inspections. The restaurant's chef is talented, but verbally abusive to staff. Many of its workers are highly trained, but they tire of picking up the slack from others who don't know what they're doing or don't seem to care about doing a good job. Small problems at the restaurant accrue. Vent fans and grease traps are clogged with gunk, boxes of supplies are stacked on the floor and line the narrow walkways, and employees are pressed to work harder and faster. Additionally, much of the kitchen's equipment is nonfunctional or out of date.

The owner of the restaurant has high ambitions for it and craves a Michelin star. They decide to invest a lot of money in top-of-the-line, computerized appliances. They also create a thick spiral-bound book of quality-ensuring policies and procedures. They have it all delivered one Saturday night after closing, then sit back and wait for incredible results.

If the owner popped into their restaurant a month later, would it be any surprise if they found nothing had changed at all—that the new tools and procedures that were introduced without explanation, training, or follow-up remained ignored and unused, and that the culture of the kitchen remained toxic? Of course not. In fact, it would be far more surprising if something *had* changed!

We can never achieve high reliability healthcare if we merely introduce safety programs—whether principles or pillars—or purchase snazzy new tools without first developing a healthy culture. High reliability healthcare must be much more than a tacked-on effort to decrease serious errors. It has to be the way an entire hospital, clinic, or organization consistently functions. It must be both systemic and perpetual. Does this relate to healthcare? Absolutely!

In a Heartbeat

When Bob was engaged in the field of cultural assessment in healthcare, he was tasked with investigating a department that was grappling with a significant number of adverse events and high turnover rates on a cardiac unit. To begin his analysis, he reviewed culture survey results and risk reports, and conducted interviews with the physicians working in that department. The situation was one of the most alarming he had encountered during his professional career.

Concurrently, he was exploring various concepts for his dissertation for his doctoral studies at Rollins College. One construct that piqued his interest was perceived organizational support, which is "the extent to which the organization values [its employees'] contributions and cares about their well-being."[80]

He was drawn to this concept when reading an article in the *McKinsey Quarterly* entitled "Great Attrition or Great Attraction? The Choice is Yours." The article revealed that the most significant factor influencing employees' decisions to leave an organization is whether they feel valued.[81] This prompted Bob to wonder if a perceived lack of support might be contributing to the high incidence of adverse events in the department. To explore this further, he decided to visit the unit in question.

While there, he had the pleasure of meeting and connecting with team member Jim. Their conversation started with casual chitchat and soon grew to story sharing. After Bob learned more about Jim's background, he began to question him about the unit's safety issues and found that he was extremely knowledgeable. Oddly, Jim's demeanor and understanding didn't align with the negative reports Bob had received. Bob wondered for a moment if he had arrived at the correct location; he was perplexed!

Bob asked Jim how long he had been working in that unit, thinking he might be a recent addition. To Bob's surprise, Jim had been a part of the unit for two years—ruling out the possibility that Jim was new and therefore not involved in the unit's troubles.

As Bob prepared to depart, he posed one final question, drawn from a validated survey related to perceived organizational support—a question that has been in use for decades: "If your organization had the opportunity to hire someone to replace you at a lower salary, would they do it?"

Jim's immediate reaction was nothing short of a transformation. His cheerful demeanor gave way to palpable anger. Without hesitation, he pointed at Bob and vehemently declared, "In a HEARTBEAT!" He added that it would take less time for the organization to replace him with someone willing to accept a lower salary than it would to bury him six feet under if he died. He criticized the organization's attempts to appease employees with pizza parties and five-dollar gift cards, describing them as insincere and artificial—even embarrassing.

With a quick shift, Jim returned to his original, jovial self and expressed his pleasure in meeting Bob. As Bob walked away, he couldn't help but feel a sense of sympathy for Jim. It became abundantly clear that a lack of perceived organizational support was a significant cause of the department's challenges with reliability and turnover.

Jim was not looking for espresso machines or ping pong tables in the break room, as one might expect from a Silicon Valley company. Rather, he wished for his company to meet basic team member needs by keeping essential supplies readily available and maintaining staffing levels high enough to deliver excellent patient care.

Inadequate staffing for a given job brings the classic chocolate episode of *I Love Lucy* to mind. In the show, Lucy and Ethel begin work at Kramer's Kandy Kitchen and are tasked with wrapping candies that continuously emerge on a conveyor belt. Though they are able to keep pace in the beginning, the increasing speed of the conveyor belt and quantity of the candies soon make it impossible for them to succeed. Ethel and Lucy do all they can to keep up or hide the evidence of their failure—including eating some chocolates and stuffing others in their hats and down their shirts.

Though it's not nearly as funny, employees who are understaffed and unsupported in real life must also devise creative solutions or workarounds to complete their tasks. In addition to the pressure of the job, these workers have the knowledge that a mistake could jeopardize their professional license, personal safety, or the safety of their patient. A significant error could even lead to legal repercussions, as happened with RaDonda Vaught.

How would an employee in such conditions assess their value to their company? Would they be inclined to go the extra mile to help the organization prevent errors? Would they stick around long or look for opportunities outside of the company?

Though organizations should be committed to continuous improvement and Six Sigma initiatives to reduce expenses, in many instances, a company's primary emphasis is on enhancing the bottom line—at any cost. In the pursuit of efficiency, hasty decisions are made and undue risks are accepted. Frequently, organizations prioritize short-term savings that make executives appear successful and meet corporate goals.

These shortsighted actions often have dire consequences: Patient safety is harmed, employee turnover increases, and the financial and legal costs to the company increase exponentially. Witnessing such situations is truly disheartening.

It Comes from the Top

As the above examples illustrate, leaders are the main drivers of culture within an organization. The best executives engage employees by instilling purpose at work, fostering an enjoyable environment, and making employees feel valued and heard. Often, a large part of their strategy is simply listening and responding, fixing problems promptly.

In *Culture Renovation: 18 Leadership Actions to Build an Unshakeable Company*, Kevin Oakes, CEO and cofounder of the Institute for Corporate Productivity, looked at more than a hundred big companies—such as Microsoft, T-Mobile, and 3M—that wanted to change their culture. One of the key things Oakes found is that if you want to change your culture, you must have complete buy-in from the CEO.[82]

Culture—whether good or bad—permeates down throughout an organization. Though a captain's ability to set the tone on a submarine with its 160 crew members is surely different than a CEO's influence on a national healthcare organization with thousands of employees, the organizational structure is similar. Both captains and CEOs must foster trust with open communication, consistent indications of caring, and a willingness to listen to and act on feedback. The standards of a high reliability organization—those five pillars that we will soon dig into—must be embedded in the culture and returned to again and again. They are the caring expectations that must be lived by on a daily basis.

Hospital CEOs must model culture-building for their VPs, and the VPs for their directors, and the directors for their managers, and so on throughout the organization. Each leader must make sure that their direct reports follow the same cultural framework and create a feeling of psychological safety among their workers.

What Is Healthcare's Ultimate Concern?

Some healthcare leaders think they must prioritize their organization's EBITDA (earnings before interest, taxes, depreciation, and amortization) above all else. "If we run out of money," they say, "we will have no healthcare organization." But those who believe this are missing the main point.

In his book, *The Hidden Power of Relentless Stewardship*, Don Jernigan, the late former president of AdventHealth and former naval officer, writes, "This bears repeating. Always view whatever metrics you employ through the lens of your mission and vision. At AdventHealth System, we use metrics not only to help us utilize our financial resources more efficiently but also to improve the service we provide to everyone who comes through our doors for medical treatment."[83] The word "balance" figures prominently in Jernigan's book. He mentions five components that all executives should keep in balance to ensure that they can fulfill their organization's specific mission. These areas include finance, quality and safety, service, market, and team, which Jernigan insists must be continually monitored all the time.[84]

In some healthcare organizations today, finance has eclipsed every other metric. In such places, quality and safety are merely talking points versus crucial areas of focus. But when organizations reduce personnel or cut corners in order to meet budget, then reliability, culture, turnover, and patient safety pay the price. This kind of focus erodes the trust employees have in their leaders and undermines the culture of the organization.

We need a healthcare culture in which the priority of every clinical and nonclinical employee is the safety and well-being of the patient. Focusing on patient care and supporting care providers is best for both patients and for business.

A Broken Relationship

An organization or a leader with the wrong focus will quickly and effectively kill a culture of caring and high reliability. When budgets get cut, staffing levels drop, and equipment is not properly maintained, it becomes impossible for workers to uphold the highest of standards. What's more, such financial decisions send a clear message to employees that the organization does not care about their needs. If an organization doesn't give its team members the tools to do their jobs correctly, it will cultivate feelings of frustration or apathy within them.

One orthopedic surgeon complained to us that the tools he was given to work with had far exceeded their recommended life expectancy and needed to be replaced. He believed the outdated tools represented a biohazard.

This doctor was highly capable and known for tackling the toughest cases. If an accident left someone with a crushed hand or multiple broken bones, he was the surgeon to call. Yet, he became increasingly disenchanted and disengaged with his healthcare system because of the lack of support he received and the number of small-order deficiencies that were continually present. He felt his environment was inhibiting his performance and ability to remain highly reliable. Though the organization did eventually provide the surgeon with updated equipment, its slow response time had already broken his trust. The talented surgeon decided to move on, hoping to find a system where he felt more supported.

The organization's decision to keep the surgical tools past their recommended preventative maintenance dates was surely a cost-saving measure—a choice that didn't account for the expense of recruiting a new orthopedic surgeon, let alone the cost to patients who may be hurt from the use of old equipment.

The Heart and Brain

As we close this chapter on culture and prepare to discuss standards, we want to emphasize the critical nature of each. Just as the heart and brain are equally vital for human survival, a healthy, trust-based culture (the heart) and clear strategies, standards, and procedures (the brain) are both critical for building a successful organization. If the heart of a healthcare system is failing—if employees don't feel trusted, valued, or heard—the outcomes of the organization will begin to fail as well. However, if an organization cares for its employees and creates a psychologically safe environment, it can set and maintain exceptional standards and achieve unmatched results.

7

THE FIVE PILLARS: CULTURALLY EXPECTED BEHAVIORS

As Admiral Rickover pondered the American military after World War II, he saw that the standard operating procedures of the day would never work for the nuclear navy.

Sailors did what they were told—no more—and they did not ask questions. They never challenged their superiors.

Rickover could not let individuals trained with such lackluster standards run his nuclear submarines. He needed people conditioned within a high reliability culture to safely operate those reactors—and he set about to create a rigorous set of standards, his watchstanding principles.

What Are the Five Pillars?

Derived from Rickover's core watchstanding principles and adapted for healthcare, the five pillars are cultural expectations that guide one's actions. They set organizational benchmarks for how to behave and, over time, impact culture.

The five pillars are *not* used to get individuals in trouble. Rather, they provide a potent tool to promote safety for both patients and workers.

As we applied the five pillars in a healthcare setting, we simplified them and created the mnemonic "**HI**gh-**F**unctioning **Q**uarter**B**ack" to make them easy to remember:

H = *Higher Level of Understanding*

I = *Integrity*

F = *Formality*

Q = *Questioning Attitude*

B = *Backup*

We're not the first to suggest that the watchstanding principles can help other organizations and industries outside of the US Navy. Bob has a colleague named Bob Koonce, for example, who cowrote the book *Extreme Operational Excellence*. Koonce spent twenty years in the navy, serving on five nuclear submarines, including one stint as commander of the USS *Key West*. After retiring from the navy in 2011, Koonce became a manager and consultant in the power industry. He teaches effective seminars for power industry personnel on how to use the watchstanding principles of high reliability to achieve operational excellence.

A quick Google search also reveals a consulting company and cybersecurity firm that have adapted their own pillars from the nuclear navy's watchstanding principles. We mention these examples to highlight the extreme utility of the watchstanding principles and to recognize their use in various industries. We've started to use them at many hospitals and have already witnessed some impressive results.

The Principles vs. the Pillars

As we've seen, there are significant differences between Weick and Sutcliffe's five principles of high reliability (the typical standard in healthcare) and our five pillars (derived from the nuclear navy's watchstanding principles). For patient safety training, we line up the five principles on the left and the five pillars on the right to compare the two approaches:

The Five Principles	**The Five Pillars**
1. Preoccupation with Failure *Be constantly concerned with failure versus success.*	1. Higher Level of Understanding *Continuously improve your knowledge on a personal level.*
2. Deference to Expertise *Value expertise and experience over title; flatten the hierarchy.*	2. Integrity *Do what you say, and do what is right when no one is looking.*
3. Sensitivity to Operations *Recognize the gap between "work as intended" versus "work that is done."*	3. Formality *Follow procedures, act with professionalism, and respect the rules.*
4. Reluctance to Simplify *Resist superficial explanations and probe deeper.*	4. A Questioning Attitude *Be vigilant and proactive when things don't seem right.*
5. Commitment to Resilience *Approach inevitable errors with an intent to detect, contain, and respond appropriately.*	5. Backup *Look beyond your own activity and take ownership to fix known defects.*

In our opinion, the five pillars are much simpler to understand and far easier for frontline healthcare workers to use in their daily care of patients than the principles. Also, while the five pillars speak to individual behavior and actions at every level of an organization, the principles are aimed at executive leadership and address the prevention of and recovery from major catastrophes. Still, for the five pillars to work—thus changing the culture—every person working in healthcare must both understand and use all five of them.

We will dedicate a chapter to each of the five pillars and explore them fully in Part Three, but first, we'll briefly describe them and offer examples from the nuclear navy.

1: Higher Level of Understanding

Admiral Rickover believed that for individuals to think critically and not act like robots, they had to fully understand the key concepts related to their jobs. He saw grasping the appropriate engineering principles as vital to the safe operation of a reactor plant.

When candidates are first accepted into the nuclear navy program, they sit with the engineers who designed the reactors. These engineers give the candidates specific physics problems to solve in order to test the candidates' understanding of engineering and math.

After six months in a nuclear power school (where attrition is high), the candidates who have passed are taken to a prototype naval nuclear reactor, not a simulation. In this hands-on training, similar to a residency program, candidates learn and become licensed to operate a reactor core.

Individuals are not done once they get certified, however. Ongoing, periodic training programs are normal and expected. Learning and maintaining a higher level of understanding is a constant process.

How does the pillar work at sea? On one of Bob's ships, a reactor scram occurred. The incident happened when the ship was running drills, pretending they had detected a torpedo in the water. When they maximized the power plant, someone made a mistake, which caused the reactor to exceed its limit by a very small amount. The reactor remained completely safe, but because it had experienced a protective action, Bob's team was required to submit an incident report. Bob and his team had to get to the root cause of why this happened.

They discovered their training program was inadequate, especially their drill-monitoring process. During the next major external audit of engineering, the effectiveness of corrective actions was scrutinized through exam reviews and personal interviews. The auditors quizzed the crew with such questions as: "Could you provide a written explanation of the heat balance equation and use thermodynamics equations to substantiate the core's pressure and temperature parameters during the incident?" The examiners' objective was to determine whether the ship's personnel genuinely possessed a thorough comprehension of the subject matter. The crew proved that they did.

A rigorous level of knowledge is crucial. How can someone question whether a procedure is correct if they don't know what the procedure fully requires? How can they offer backup?

Critical thinking is a foundational skill in every area of life, and you can't have critical thinking unless you have a higher level of understanding. That's why we place "a higher level of understanding" as the first pillar in high reliability healthcare.

2: Integrity

In the nuclear navy, integrity gets split into two areas. First, *personal* integrity means doing what's right even when no one is looking. Of course, an individual must have ample opportunity to understand an organization's standards and requirements before they can fairly be held accountable to them. But when the culture of an organization ensures that each individual is fully aware of what is expected, abiding by those expectations then becomes a matter of personal integrity.

When Bob first took command of the USS *Texas,* a rash of sailors were not following procedure. The *Texas* was a struggling ship with low morale and a significant number of safety issues. Bob knew he couldn't hold his men accountable until he had clearly spelled out his expectations. So, every Friday, he drilled his crew on those standards. One of them was procedural compliance: all initial conditions met, all precautions met, with each step understood and followed. Bob had his crew repeat the definition to him every Friday.

For about a month, things began to improve. The *Texas* had "pre-underways" to verify that all equipment ran properly. Bob had to know that if the sub needed something while at sea, it was fully prepared. But one day, as the ship was readying to get underway, an incident occurred.

One item on the pre-underway list called for the crew to start up the emergency diesel generator, a huge Caterpillar engine used to supplement electric power in the event the reactor went down. The day before the sub got underway, Bob received a report that the diesel engine had shut down upon startup.

Because the cultural standard for dealing with any issue was to conduct an investigation appropriate to the severity of it, no one said, "Oh, let's try starting the engine again to see what happens." Rather, a complete review of the problem was conducted to find what had gone wrong.

The following day, Bob was briefed by the engineer officer about the investigation, which highlighted a temperature issue. Ideally, the lubricating oil should maintain a constant temperature of ninety degrees, but on the day of the test, it had become colder, causing the lube oil temperature to drop to seventy degrees. That cooler temperature made the oil more viscous, causing the back pressure to exceed an automatic shutdown limit and consequently shutting down the diesel generator.

Bob didn't rail at the sailors or punish them for their error. Rather, he celebrated the learning opportunity with them, then reviewed the expected standards and discussed the mistake.

"Petty Officer Smith," he said, "what's the definition of procedural compliance?" Smith recited it as a seasoned sailor: "All initial conditions are met."

To the duty officer who authorized the maintenance, Bob said, "What is the definition of procedural compliance?" The man replied, "All initial conditions are met."

"So," Bob continued, "if the procedure here says that when starting the diesel generator, the lube oil shall be at ninety degrees, why was it at seventy?" The duty officer had no answer.

At that moment, Bob could have justly disciplined the men responsible. But he didn't *have* to. That one reminder of procedure and accountability was enough. The sailors involved already felt they had disappointed the ship. They had raised their hands and owned their mistake rather than making excuses for it. In return, they didn't need—or receive—further punishment.

A healthy culture produces this kind of personal integrity and two-way trust.

The second kind of integrity is *organizational* integrity. An organization must give an employee the proper tools and resources to perform their job the right way.

When Bob was commodore of Submarine Squadron 7, he held authority over a fleet of nuclear fast-attack submarines. His responsibilities included overseeing the certification, equipping, and officer training of these ten *Los Angeles*–class submarines. Each of the subs' commanding officers reported directly to him.

During this time, an issue of organizational integrity occurred. One of Bob's commanding officers brought a concern to him: "A petty officer neglected his maintenance duties, claiming he'd completed them when he actually hadn't. I intend to take corrective action by removing him from my ship."

Since this would have been detrimental to the petty officer's career, Bob wished to slow down and look into the matter further. He wondered if there were any issues regarding the ship's organizational integrity. It's quite simple to attribute all the blame to an untrustworthy employee, but did the petty officer comprehend the demands of his role? Were there obstacles hindering his ability to fulfill them?

Bob discovered that the sailor's daily routine involved reporting to work at 7:00 a.m. and spending six hours idly waiting for a list of maintenance tasks. This was not due to the sailor's lack of motivation, but rather a result of a culture characterized by excessive supervision, work inefficiencies, and a strict requirement for authorization from the commanding officer for even minor tasks. The CO's policies caused a bottleneck. Every sailor on board lacked the freedom to initiate projects without approval from the CO himself. This led to extreme inefficiencies because no one person could approve every task on a submarine in a timely fashion.

Each day at noon, senior officers and senior enlisted crew members convened to determine the maintenance tasks that needed to be accomplished by the end of the day. During this meeting, the captain granted authorization for the afternoon and nighttime work. Once approval was obtained, the chief petty officer in charge of the division would approach the sailor around 1:00 p.m. and inform him, "These tasks are essential and must be completed before you can leave." Finishing the maintenance typically occupied the sailor's time into the evening, keeping him from returning home until 8:00 p.m.

After all the days at sea and the in-port duty days that required overnight stays, the numerous long days and late nights were just too much for the sailor's wife. She had reached her breaking point. One evening, when the petty officer arrived home at 8:00 p.m. once again, his wife handed him their crying baby and expressed her frustration: "Dinner is cold. I'm tired of eating alone, exhausted from being home all day with our baby, and I am fed up with the navy. You're sleeping on the couch. And if you arrive home late one more time, I'm leaving you."

The sailor was in an unwinnable situation. If he admitted the maintenance was not completed, the chief in charge would have mandated that he work additional hours. Driven by deep concern for his wife and the state of their marriage, the sailor decided to skip maintenance tasks that posed no harm to equipment or individuals. Though he falsified reports, the petty officer confessed to the truth when the deception was uncovered.

The incident indicated to Bob that the CO had created a bad culture. He hadn't given the petty officer an opportunity to work efficiently. It was a failure of organizational integrity.

Bob assisted the commanding officer in enhancing work efficiencies, which fostered a culture of compassion and strengthened organizational integrity. Ultimately, the petty officer was permitted to stay on board.

3: Formality

Formality refers to both procedure and communication. There are formal ways to do certain procedures, and there are formal ways to communicate within the groups doing those procedures.

On a nuclear sub, each valve has a number, such as charging 5 (CH-5). All primary valve operations are directed from a maneuvering area. The engineering officer of the watch (EOOW) will say to the engineering watch supervisor (EWS), "Open CH-5." The electrical operator (EO), also acting as a phone talker in the maneuvering area, will report back the order to the EOOW. The EO will then, through the sound-powered phones, say, "EWS open CH-5." The EWS will acknowledge the order and direct the valve operator to open CH-5. The operator will then point to the valve and say out loud, "Opening CH-5." Once CH-5 is open, he will announce, "CH-5 is open." Then a report of CH-5 being open will be communicated to maneuvering, where a status board will be updated. The EOOW follows a set procedure to direct the whole operation.

These repeat backs are one example of formality within the nuclear navy. They are simple, reliable processes that confirm accurate communication and reduce errors. We also consider "formality" to include written policies and consistent adherence to them. The sailors' failure to ensure that all initial conditions were met, in our earlier example, was not just a failure of personal integrity; it was a failure of formality as well.

4: A Questioning Attitude

When a situation doesn't seem right, you should ask questions. Rickover encouraged his team to be ever questioning. He agreed with the words of author Philip Wylie, "Ignorance is not bliss—it is oblivion."[85] Rickover urged navy personnel to become better informed and learn from others' mistakes, regardless of their place in the organizational hierarchy. He said,

"Free discussion requires an atmosphere unembarrassed by any suggestion of authority or even respect."[86]

A questioning attitude democratizes safety; that's why crew members on a nuclear sub are both trained and encouraged to have one.

5: Backup

Members of an organization must look beyond their own activity, pay attention to issues their team may be facing, and do what they can to resolve those issues. They must back one another up.

Bob remembers when the backup offered by the assistant navigator on board his submarine directly led to the success of a critical mission. Tasked with monitoring a specific combatant submarine, the USS *Texas* had to guess the path the ship would take through a narrow, winding sea pass and plan its tracking route accordingly. Like an interstate's exit ramps, there were only certain places a sub could leave the passage. Based on width and depth, Bob and his navigation team estimated that there was an 80 percent chance their adversary would take "exit A" and a 20 percent chance the ship would take "exit B." After drawing up plans for either scenario, Bob was just about to move his team on to the execution phase when the assistant navigator stopped him. "Captain, wait," the sailor said. "I was doing research and found another possible exit."

The option the sailor discovered through his own initiative was shallow, narrow, and unlikely. But he'd found evidence that the route *had* been used in the past. Bob didn't discount it. He decided there was a 1 percent chance the sub would take "exit C," so he planned for that scenario as well.

And guess what happened.

Of course, the combatant ship took exit C. With a response plan in place, the *Texas* was able to continue to track the sub and complete its mission successfully. The backup of one sailor had made all the difference.

Looking Ahead

Now that we have had a brief overview of the five pillars, we will spend a chapter unpacking each one and giving specific healthcare examples of them in action. We have no doubt that the five pillars can save healthcare a great deal of pain, suffering, and loss, because we've already seen them begin to work their magic.

PART THREE

APPLYING THE FIVE PILLARS

8

A HIGHER LEVEL OF UNDERSTANDING

When London's Great Fire of 1666 destroyed St. Paul's Cathedral, famed architect Christopher Wren was commissioned to rebuild it. One day, he came upon three workers he hadn't met before and asked them each a question: "What are you doing?" The first man answered that he was cutting a stone. The second said he was earning a wage. But the third worker said, "I am helping Sir Christopher Wren to build his great cathedral."[87]

Seeing the bigger picture makes a difference, doesn't it? Those who have a higher level of understanding about what they're doing tend to do a better job.

Clinicians must have the technical expertise to successfully complete whatever work lies before them. They must be able to think critically about their situation in order to respond effectively to the huge number of variations that exist in each human body.

Great outcomes begin with an increasing ability to translate and apply technical knowledge. Team members must continually improve their level of knowledge and then routinely share the lessons they learn.

An Example from the Nuclear Navy

The USS *Texas* received orders to submerge beneath the North Pole to certify the new *Virginia*-class submarine for Arctic operations. The sub had undergone a complete engineering redesign, including how it captured and displaced carbon dioxide. In the past, CO_2 scrubbers took the gas out of the submarine using an absorbing chemical; it was a closed loop. The captured CO_2 then would be displaced overboard, using positive displacement reciprocating pumps.

In the *Los Angeles*-class submarines, the CO2 gas was discharged near the machinery room, while on the *Virginia* class, it was discharged in another location that featured longer piping subjected to sea temperature. Heaters were designed to make sure the gas didn't freeze, since frozen gas can't get discharged. Unfortunately, the heater capacity design was inadequate.

Never before had a *Virginia*-class submarine gone into such frigid waters. The *Texas* went to periscope depth, saw the ice line, and went down to start its transit under the ice. At about two o'clock in the morning, right after the sub had started sailing in Arctic waters, someone woke up Bob. "Captain," he said, "the CO2 scrubbers are discharging inboard. Something's wrong with them." Carbon dioxide levels on the ship had begun to rise, a fatal problem if not remedied quickly.

Because they were under the polar ice cap, they could not seek advice from higher authorities. The crew had forty-eight hours to solve the issue themselves before the *Texas* would have to turn back, abort the transit, and fail the mission. Bob's team got to work. These crew members had a higher level of understanding and knew they had to look for a different way to discharge the carbon dioxide overboard.

A very talented senior chief petty officer approached Bob and said, "Captain, I think we have an alternate path. Clearly, the heater capacity is not sufficient. I'm going to break this piping and connect it to the main seawater piping—which is already heated—and just discharge it into the overboard piping."

The senior chief and his team had analyzed the material needs, conducted a hose test, and ensured the feasibility of the suggested solution. Though there was no established protocol for this particular situation, the senior chief ensured Bob that it would meet all submarine safety standards.

Bob granted permission, and the team implemented its solution, discharging the gas safely overboard.

Because the senior chief had a higher level of understanding of how carbon dioxide was discharged overboard, he was able to devise an alternate way to get the job done. The fix enabled the *Texas* to continue its mission without turning back or having to abort.

What Can This Pillar Look Like in Healthcare?

Remembering the answers Christopher Wren gathered from the builders of St. Paul's Cathedral, one wonders how healthcare workers would respond to similar questions about their jobs.

Nurses must frequently insert a hollow needle into the vein of a patient's arm to introduce a fluid of some kind. If you were to ask a nurse, "What are you doing?" they might say, "I'm starting an IV." And that would be accurate.

A second nurse might answer the same question by replying, "I'm delivering fluid and medication intended to get to this patient's vital organs, which will help to heal them." This nurse's answer shows they have a higher level of clinical understanding than the first nurse.

If you approached a third nurse and asked, "What are you doing?" they might answer, "I'm helping to extend this patient's life." This third answer is especially interesting because it shows this nurse has an understanding of purpose as well as procedure. They're not merely concerned with completing a task; they want to make sure their patient has the best possible chance to enjoy a long life. Grasping the overarching purpose and end goal is the first thing a higher level of understanding requires.

Next is the effort to continually improve one's level of knowledge. For example, every nurse trained in nursing school learns how to start an IV, but knowing how to do it is not enough. A nurse who provides IV access to a patient as part of their daily job must maintain that skill by practicing it often. The easy "sticks" go well if proper technique is followed. For the difficult sticks—a neonate, a dehydrated elderly person, or a patient who has abused their veins—nurses must improve their knowledge and skill set by learning advanced techniques and/or using newer assist tools, such as a handheld ultrasound.

The final step to gaining a higher level of understanding in healthcare involves encouraging team members to routinely share lessons they've learned so that others can also increase their level of knowledge. It is particularly important to share the difficult lessons learned from tragic events to prevent similar future occurrences.

Years ago, a devastating loss revealed a critical shortcoming. A baby died at a hospital, primarily because the nurse monitoring the baby during delivery didn't know how to properly read the TOCO strip chart (the horizontal display showing the hills and valleys of the fetal heartbeat associated with labor contractions). She saw the vital signs indicating a struggling baby, but because she lacked a higher level of understanding regarding the TOCO monitor, she didn't take the actions required to notify others, who could possibly have saved the infant's life. The problem arose because she hadn't been trained properly (an issue of organizational integrity—see the next chapter).

Rather than merely giving the nurse some didactic training to verify that the problem had been corrected, a supervisor required the nurse to pass a test. By earning a specific minimum score, the nurse had to prove that she knew how to recognize and act properly when similar irregular indications signaled another baby in distress. The supervisor then shared this difficult lesson learned with her colleagues.

From that point on, to continue working on that floor, all nurses had to be certified on the TOCO monitor at specific, regular intervals. By making this change, not only did the nurse involved in the incident gain a higher level of understanding, but so did the rest of the unit's caregivers.

Retraining should be interactive and measured. It is not enough for a clinician to passively watch educational videos or lectures. An increased level of understanding must be verified. In many cases, specific skills and knowledge should be determined through testing. Does the individual have a high enough level of understanding to be certified?

While we would like to see more testing done in a number of areas, we are thankful for the verification standards that *do* exist in healthcare. All doctors and nurses involved in direct patient care are required to maintain advanced cardiac life support (ACLS) certification. ACLS provides everyone with the standard-of-care approach to a cardiac arrest. One checks for a pulse, activates "code blue," administers an electrical shock when indicated, starts chest compressions, secures an airway, and delivers appropriate medications.

The critical component for patients in ventricular fibrillation (VFIB), a fatal arrhythmia, is to shock with a defibrillator in asynchronous mode stat (from the Latin *statim*, meaning "immediately"). Some patients are in a less fatal but unstable cardiac rhythm, such as atrial fibrillation with a rapid ventricular response. For these patients, cardioversion is necessary to restore a stable heartbeat. The SYNC button of the defibrillator must be selected so the machine will delay the electric shock long enough to read and synchronize with the patient's heart rhythm.

A few years ago, a patient undergoing cardioversion needed the second kind of treatment. The cardiologist leading the procedure called out "all clear" and "synchronous," but failed to activate the SYNC mode. The patient went into VFIB and cardiac arrest, from which the team resuscitated him. In a few days, the man walked out of the hospital completely healthy, but things could have turned out very differently. Fortunately, this patient and his wife now share their experience at patient safety academies.

The cardiologist lacked a higher level of understanding of the ACLS training and was not familiar with the specific model of defibrillator used. Not only did the cardiologist receive refresher training, but he also had to demonstrate hands-on proficiency in cardioversion. Further, every cardiologist and cardiac nurse performing the procedure system-wide underwent the same training, also having to demonstrate that they had the expertise and higher level of understanding required to deliver the lifesaving procedure.

Level of knowledge is the bedrock for training a team. If your people don't know what to do or why they're doing it, they can never be truly effective. In fact, a lack of knowledge can cause mistakes and lead to serious consequences. Organizations MUST have an effective training program to ensure that everyone on their team has a base level of knowledge to do their job correctly and perform to a standard of excellence that patients can rely on.

We often hear managers say that the best way to learn is by actually doing the job, and we don't disagree. But that's no substitute for a formal training program that includes on-the-job training, ongoing testing, and continuing education. This ensures a certain level of expertise that won't decay over time. HROs encourage mastery and empower their employees to achieve it.

9

INTEGRITY

The second pillar is "integrity," which carries responsibility at both a personal and organizational level. First, personal integrity refers to an individual doing what is right, regardless of personal cost or recognition. Organizational integrity, on the other hand, refers to an organization doing what is right for its employees. It asks whether the company is creating the right environment, offering support, training, and tools, and doing all it can to ensure its employees can perform their jobs effectively.

Again, let's look at how this plays out in the nuclear navy, and then return to see what it can look like in healthcare.

How to Fix an Oil Leak on a Sub

One day aboard the USS *Texas*, a crew member noticed an oil leak on a hull valve after the submarine had submerged. According to naval regulations, such maintenance tasks must be carried out with dual-valve protection. If only a single valve were used and it turned out to be faulty, it could result in oil spreading throughout the entire compartment—potentially endangering the crew. For this reason, the use of a single valve for protection is normally discouraged unless there are specific operational reasons that necessitate it.

In this particular situation, opting for a two-valve replacement would mean repositioning torpedoes, a process that would consume a minimum of three to four hours. Properly executing the replacement with two valves would entail a significant amount of additional work.

The ship's chief looked at Bob and said, "Captain, I can take that O-ring and replace it in ten minutes. Give me the word and we'll do it." The chief envisioned a quick work-around.

"No, Chief," Bob replied. "I know that this is a simple repair with minimal-to-no risk, but that type of work-around doesn't follow procedure. Even if no one else found out, and everything went well, it wouldn't be the right thing to do. If I gave you authorization, it would set an extremely bad precedent and could potentially lead to harm. I know you're trying to save time and I really appreciate the offer, but this is not the right thing to do."

Bob wanted his chief to understand that following standard procedure would not only help to ensure nothing went wrong—it would shield him from liability if something did. Bob told him, "If you follow the procedure and do everything right, you are completely covered. You have insurance. But once you violate your integrity and do something that you know isn't authorized, you have no protection from blame." Personal integrity protects both the organization and the individual.

What Does the Integrity Pillar Look Like in Healthcare?

Integrity in healthcare means following the five pillars, doing what we say we will do—being accountable—, doing what's right, regardless of whether someone's looking. It also means we don't cut corners, even if we think it will save some time.

Frequently in healthcare, there's the temptation to work around requirements to meet a needed purpose. Unfortunately, the more this type of behavior occurs, the more accepted it becomes. It tends to happen in the emergency department (ED) much more than in the operating room, but throughout a hospital or clinic, work-arounds can become the norm.

We must develop a culture in which shortcuts and duct-tape fixes are the rare exception.

When employees, out of necessity, independently change a standard procedure or "fix" a malfunctioning piece of equipment by employing some creative engineering, they may applaud their own ingenuity. In truth, however, these unapproved deviations from formal procedures indicate a failure of integrity and could have disastrous effects.

We shudder to imagine what could have happened recently if one of our hospital transporters had decided to take a shortcut rather than diligently following protocol.

Using the wheelchair he'd been given, the transporter escorted a patient from their room to the MRI intake area for a scheduled MRI procedure. The employee followed procedure and waited for an MRI technician to inspect the wheelchair. Though it would have been faster to forgo the final safety check, the transporter displayed unwavering personal integrity by patiently waiting. This cautious approach proved essential, as it was discovered that the wheelchair was, in fact, not MRI safe. Had the transporter not chosen the right—though less convenient—course of action, the wheelchair could have posed a dangerous threat, potentially harming the patient.

The Substitution Test

Normalized deviation typically starts to happen when resources get tight and workers have no time to fix a problem correctly. One work-around leads to another. And at some point, almost inevitably, the unit will suffer a catastrophic event as a result.

Too often, healthcare organizations don't give their employees everything they need to do their jobs properly, yet when something goes wrong, they hold their employees accountable for the incident without taking equal responsibility for the organization's own culpability. Organizational integrity and fairness mean that the organization habitually sets up its workers for success.

Our healthcare system uses an important tool to determine if a caregiver's error was out of the norm and entirely their fault, or if a lack of organizational integrity contributed to the incident. We call this tool "the substitution test." If an employee does something that causes harm, we interview three equally trained individuals to learn how each of them would react under an identical set of circumstances. If none of the three would choose to follow the same path as the employee in question, then the individual is likely at fault and needs to be dealt with appropriately.

But if at least one says, "I *absolutely* would have done the same thing," then we know the problem was not with the individual who caused harm. More than likely, it was an organizational issue, which must be investigated further and corrected with appropriate process changes.

Even if a clinician does something like falsifying a patient's record, it may not be a matter of poor personal integrity so much as an onerous system that sets workers up to fail. Organizational integrity means we must give our people the opportunity, tools, and support they need to perform at the highest level.

Set up for Failure?

An oncology center faced numerous operational issues that posed significant safety risks for patients already battling life-threatening illnesses. It was crucial to ensure that these problems did not hinder their fight.

When we asked about the team's primary concerns, one caregiver mentioned a computer that had been nonfunctional for months. "Why is it taking so long to repair this computer?" she asked with frustration. "I believe it can be fixed within four hours."

The useless computer took up room in an already-crowded treatment area. Each time a patient's information had to be entered, an additional clinician working on a laptop borrowed from another area would have to squeeze into the space to enter the data.

The unit's manager objected to the caregiver's suggestion: "We're upgrading our EMR [electronic medical record] software, and that's the number one IT priority for the corporation right now. We don't have time or resources to fix that little computer."

We pushed back. "Let us be the squeaky wheel here because this is directly affecting safety. We strongly suggest you fix the computer."

"Unfortunately," the manager replied, "we've been told by corporate that nothing will interfere with the upgrade."

"We don't care," we answered. "Either find someone internally to fix this or hire a contractor. It's unacceptable to be unable to support this team's vital safety concerns because of an EMR upgrade."

The EMR upgrade had already cost too much, and leaders throughout the organization felt enormous pressure to control the bottom line. This mindset—cutting costs even at the expense of safety—is never right but would certainly have been more understandable if the corporation were at risk of going out of business. But such was not the case.

As a result of this unnecessary pressure to keep costs low, resources were diverted from other areas to fund the upgrade, and work-arounds became common.

Workers feared what would happen if they hurt the bottom line, and they felt scared to speak up. They stayed quiet about problems they observed and simply hoped that nothing bad would come of them. Essentially, the caregivers gambled with their patients' safety.

Another significant hazard at the oncology center was the manager's failure to follow protocol. Though she was required to periodically monitor and document her team members as they washed their hands, donned and doffed sterile protective garments, etc., she could produce no documentation. *None.*

She and her team were also well below standards in their knowledge of how to properly clean the unit.

Though it seemed evident that the manager was at fault, it was unfair to hold her fully accountable until we had examined the integrity of the organization. Had the system provided the manager the training and support she needed? Were systemic deficiencies outside of her control setting her up for failure? How could we blame the manager and her team if they never learned what "right" looked like?

It is only after an organization has set and ingrained standards, addressed issues, and provided workers with the tools they need to succeed that a failure of integrity on a personal level can truly be considered.

Following our intervention, the computer in the oncology department was repaired, and standards were enhanced through employee training and feedback, leadership coaching, and increased care for the staff. As the numerous vulnerabilities were addressed, substantial improvements in safety margins were realized.

Organizational Integrity Goes Further

Organizational integrity is not only demonstrated through the equipment and training provided to staff, but also through the way a company cares for the mental well-being of its employees. We came across a perfect example of this type of support in healthcare during the height of the COVID pandemic.

In system-wide surveys, employees at one hospital facility consistently reported much lower burnout scores than employees in sister facilities. Their staff retention rate was also the highest by far—nearly double the average retention score. We searched but could not find external reasons for these results. The staffing levels, workload, quality of tools and facility, opportunities to give feedback, etc., were all comparable to the other campuses.

In hopes of discovering the secret, we started soliciting stories from the hospital's employees. That's when we learned about COVID nurse Angela.

The physical, mental, and emotional strain of the pandemic was difficult for all, but undoubtedly, it was the most trying for frontline caregivers. Angela had grown weary of the long hours, the heartache of watching patients die, and all the unknowns that accompanied the crisis. The isolation she felt was the final straw. As a nurse who worked directly with

COVID patients, Angela was required to wear special protective gear. The garments not only guarded her from the virus but also scared away humans. No one would ride the elevator with Angela or sit with her in the cafeteria. People would change direction when they saw her coming down the hallway. She felt isolated and unvalued.

Angela decided to post about her experience on the digital communication boards at her facility. "This is difficult enough," Angela wrote. "I don't need to be shunned by my coworkers."

The campus's leadership team learned what Angela had written and responded quickly. The next day, physicians and executives gathered together in the intensive care unit to present each COVID nurse with a gift and a card, as well as a videotaped message of love and thanks from the entire support staff of the hospital.

When we heard Angela's story and others like it, we realized that the facility's low burnout and high retention scores could be directly attributed to its culture and organizational integrity. Not only did the facility's heartfelt response to Angela's struggle demonstrate integrity in that moment, but the fact that she felt safe venting her feelings on the communication boards demonstrated it as well. Angela felt psychologically safe to speak out, which showed the leadership's responses of the past had fostered a culture of trust.

Integrity of this type on both a personal and organizational level must be embedded into the culture of any organization seeking to become an HRO.

10

FORMALITY

The third pillar is "formality," which means that rules are respected, procedures are followed, and work-arounds are avoided. Information is communicated and reported clearly using techniques such as repeat backs to ensure that all parties understand and agree with the next steps. Teams also have standard procedures and processes from which they do not deviate.

A Formality Check in the Nuclear Navy

In the control center of a nuclear attack submarine, the newest-reporting and least-experienced sailors take on the role of the watch messenger. This messenger aids the chief of the watch in performing daily tasks. Among the responsibilities of the watch messenger is ensuring that the upcoming watchstanders are up on time. The messenger accomplishes this by physically visiting the bunks of individual crew members with a flashlight and gently waking them, essentially serving as an alarm clock. While this role may not be crucial to the immediate safety of the ship, it plays an important part in maintaining the daily routine on board.

One day, Bob overheard the chief of the watch say to the messenger, "Go wake up Chief Smith.'" The watch messenger walked away without repeating the command. Bob immediately entered the control room and, stopping the messenger, said, "Hang on, Chief, why didn't you make sure the messenger gave a repeat back? Why didn't you make sure he said, 'Go wake up Chief Smith, aye'?"

When he received no answer, Bob continued, "Do you know why this is important? Repeat backs are standard procedure, and consistently following procedure is part of the culture we're setting. Young sailors must become so used to using repeat backs every day that they use them automatically in an emergency—when doing so is critical. If that messenger doesn't remember to say, 'Go wake Chief Smith, aye' now, he's not going to remember to repeat back when it matters."

It's not only the nuclear navy that requires its personnel to repeat back procedures. Jeff clearly recalls the same practice of formality in communication among naval aviators. Pilot one says, "I have control," while the second pilot repeats back, "Check, you have control." Jeff often heard the same kind of repeat back in helicopters. "I have the stick," says one pilot. "You have the stick," repeats the other pilot. Formality in communication helps military teams ensure their own safety.

Formality in the nuclear navy is not only about using formal patterns of communication, however; it's also about following formal procedures.

One day, when the USS *Texas* was in port, a crew member discovered that a bearing on a main water pump needed to be replaced. A delay in departure would jeopardize important aspects of the ship's next mission.

The chief said to Bob, "Captain, this is important. I can do this. We don't have to rely on a maintenance facility, because it takes two days for them to plan it, get the paperwork done, and so forth. We can be done quicker if we fix it ourselves."

"Are you sure you can do this?" Bob asked.

"Absolutely," came the reply.

As the chief and his team prepared to do the repair, Bob said to them, "Listen, this is a new procedure for this *Virginia*-class submarine. I doubt this has ever been done before. If you have *any* deviations from the approved procedure and the bearing fails again, they will investigate to see what we did or didn't do. I care about you and don't want you to sacrifice your personal integrity to ensure we get to sea on time. It's not worth it."

As it happened, about six hours later, the team encountered a challenge when they discovered that the procedure had been inaccurately written. They sought clarification from Naval Sea Systems Command in Washington, DC, the authors of the procedure, and received formal approval for a revised procedure. The maintenance was then carried out correctly and the ship was able to execute its mission on schedule.

Bob's team sensed urgency, but unlike the CO2 example from chapter 8, lives were not at stake. Bypassing formal instructions and authorization in this case could jeopardize their credibility and lead to other negative consequences. Bob demonstrated his concern for their welfare by insisting that their integrity and well-being took precedence over the mission.

Formality in Healthcare

Formality in healthcare parallels what exists in the nuclear navy. Healthcare, too, needs both formality in communication and formality in procedure. Let's briefly look at each.

1. *Formality in communication*

   First, formality means precise communication, particularly in crucial settings.

   A frustrated orthopedic surgeon recently shared with us the significant headache arising from not practicing a simple repeat back. During a surgical procedure, the doctor had requested a size-five implant, but the technician did not repeat back the request and mistakenly provided a size six. The surgeon, occupied with other aspects of the procedure, relied on the technician to provide what had been requested. It was only after the wrong implant had been inserted that the surgeon realized the error. Corrective action had to be taken, which meant increased time in surgery and additional trauma and damage to the patient's joint.

If the surgical team had practiced repeat backs, the unfortunate incident could have likely been avoided.

Of course, it's possible the scrub tech could have repeated back the correct implant and then handed the surgeon the wrong one, but it's far more likely that they would pick up and deliver the right implant after correctly echoing the surgeon's command.

No process guarantees perfection; human beings make mistakes, after all. But we make far fewer mistakes when we follow formality in communication.

The Joint Commission reported communication failures as the root cause of most sentinel (adverse) events.[88] A formal communication tool, such as the I-PASS mnemonic developed by pediatricians Christopher Landrigan and Amy Starmer, can help minimize communication failures. I-PASS formalizes communication between clinicians during change of shifts when patients are handed off to a new team of caregivers. By discussing or documenting each item of I-PASS (**I**llness severity, **P**atient information, **A**ction list, **S**ituational awareness and contingency plans, and **S**ynthesis by receiver), caregivers going off duty can be certain they have covered their bases and thoroughly communicated all pertinent patient information to the new shift. I-PASS streamlines workflow, prevents harm, and improves patient care.[89]

Consider the difference formality makes to a code blue team that deals with high-stress, life-threatening events on a daily basis. Though the team members may only have time for the briefest of communications in the midst of a medical emergency, they can and *should* communicate at length before a call begins. A clear understanding beforehand of who will perform each role—checking the airway, starting the IV, defibrillating the patient—will prevent confusion later. This formality in communication will help to elicit the best performance from the code blue team and ensure the safest, most positive outcome for the patient.

In addition to practicing communication, emergency clinicians must rehearse scenarios, following the appropriate process until each step is ingrained and automatic. This leads us to the second aspect of formality.

2. *Formality in procedure*

   Formality in healthcare could also be called "procedural compliance." Compliance is making sure that all specified procedures are followed and completed. In practice, this means: "Respect the rules, follow the procedures, and avoid work-arounds."

Many of healthcare's problems stem from a violation of multiple pillars at once. In the last chapter, for example, we highlighted how work-arounds typically violate the second pillar, integrity. But they also violate this third pillar, formality. They represent a deviation from approved procedure. While work-arounds usually save time in the moment, in the long run they too often lead to a sudden catastrophe—especially when multiple work-arounds combine.

The standard of care when doing a kidney biopsy is to mark with a pen the laterality (right or left) on the patient's back before the procedure begins. If someone takes a shortcut and just drapes the intended side without putting ink to skin, the patient might shift position, and through inattention to detail, the wrong side could be biopsied.

Time-outs—or at least, effective time-outs—are not conducted consistently in some areas of healthcare. An effective time-out prior to surgery requires all participants in the OR to be present and to fully participate: the surgeon, anesthesiologist, surgical nurse, and scrub tech. They not only need to be engaged and focused, but they also must use a standardized surgical safety checklist before starting anesthesia, making the first cut, or moving the patient to recovery. According to the Joint Commission, 10 percent of surveys carried out in hospitals, critical access centers, and ambulatory accreditation programs that offer surgical services discovered issues related to deficiencies in the time-out procedure.[90]

If we truly want healthcare to become highly reliable across the board, these requirements must be followed. In our opinion, this represents just one of the critical elements that, if addressed, could enhance safety standards on a national scale.

In the US, the single largest payer of healthcare is the federal government. Centers for Medicare and Medicaid Services (CMS) controls 1.75 *trillion* dollars of healthcare spent yearly.[91] Every healthcare facility in the United States that receives payment for providing care to patients covered by CMS is required to adhere to the Conditions of Participation (CoP) and maintain health and safety standards to safeguard the well-being of beneficiaries. If CMS were more prescriptive in its CoPs about using formal communication and formal processes, then the accrediting institutions, such as the Joint Commission, Det Norske Veritas (DNV-GL), or the American Osteopathic Association (AOA) Healthcare Facilities Accreditation Program (HFAP), would be compelled to ensure that the CoPs regarding communication and processes were being met during ongoing hospital accreditation visits.

We also need a formal documentation process to accompany any investigation of a serious mistake. We can't depend on individual memory to recall what went wrong and why because memories quickly fade, and individuals leave organizations or move on to other roles. We must have a written record.

Each hospital should follow a formal process to address incidents of actual harm to patients, as well as potential harm and near misses. These events should be managed in a standardized way and reported to a Patient Safety Organization (PSO).

Authorized by the Patient Safety and Quality Improvement Act of 2005 and signed into law by President George W. Bush, PSOs analyze data that is voluntarily submitted by healthcare providers in order to improve the quality of healthcare and patient safety.[92]

Formality of documentation both preserves helpful processes and eliminates inadequate ones. If someone tries a new procedure and it turns out we want to learn from that experience, having a codified process will allow for it to be accurately replicated. Conversely, if a new attempt turns out badly, it helps to write that down as well so others won't repeat the same process. Documentation also helps maintain alignment between the mission, vision, and values of the organization.

Numerous medical errors often stem from a lack of adherence to established protocols. For instance, within the standard workflow, a team might have been tasked with reviewing diagnostic images or retrieving specific data from a computer system. However, when they encountered difficulties accessing images from an outpatient setting, they opted to proceed without the imaging. Another example might be a surgeon who believed their knowledge was sufficient enough to allow them to bypass the prescribed procedure.

While shortcuts like these may occasionally allow healthcare professionals to save time, the potentially catastrophic consequences that can result from neglecting formal procedures render such risk-taking unacceptable.

Communication, systems, and checklists work together to greatly increase our rates of success and degree of safety. But a word of caution: while formality is important, critical thinking is vital. If a procedure isn't working well, no one should mindlessly follow its dictates. They should feel free to suggest an improvement or new process. Just as Landrigan and Starmer saw a need and developed I-PASS to address that need, caregivers with a higher level of understanding can voice their concerns and help to ensure their systems are utilizing the safest, most effective processes possible.

11

A QUESTIONING ATTITUDE

One could argue that the watchstanding principle that proved most critical to changing the military culture of the 1950s was what we call "pillar four," a questioning attitude. For decades, soldiers, sailors, and airmen alike had been ordered, "Do what you're told. Don't ask questions. Don't challenge your superiors."

Admiral Hyman G. Rickover knew that such an unbending, harsh hierarchical culture would destroy the nuclear navy that he so desperately wanted to build. Instead, he taught his recruits to have a questioning attitude. He expected them and even required them, regardless of their rank, to speak up when they believed they had seen something not quite right. He demanded that they question any action or procedure that they believed could cause harm.

Rickover declared, "One must create the ability in his staff to generate clear, forceful arguments for opposing viewpoints as well as for their own. Open discussions and disagreements must be encouraged, so that all sides of an issue are fully explored."[93]

On the Lookout

During Bob's time as the executive officer on board the USS *La Jolla*, a *Los Angeles*-class, fast-attack submarine, the ship was on deployment in the western Pacific.

At 2:00 a.m., when the CO was in bed asleep, Bob, then thirty-five years old, was the senior person on board in charge of the ship's safety and operations. The *La Jolla* was cruising on the surface, en route to a port called Chinhae in South Korea. The journey involved a lengthy surface transit, characterized by significant congestion caused by dozens of small fishing boats ranging in size from thirty- to forty-foot vessels to much smaller ones whose intrepid Korean occupants ventured farther offshore in pursuit of fish.

A moonless night had plunged the sub into complete darkness except for a masthead light and a submarine identification beacon that emitted a flashing yellow signal (intended to alert other vessels to the *La Jolla*'s presence and prompt them to steer clear). The beacon's light, while essential for safety, also hindered the *La Jolla*'s visibility, making it challenging to spot potential obstacles.

Two other officers had joined Bob on the bridge: the officer of the deck responsible for navigation and ship operation, and a lookout tasked with identifying and reporting hazards. Due to the utter darkness, the lookout had trouble seeing ahead. The *La Jolla* had two radar systems, a primary and a backup system. The primary radar, integrated into the submarine by the US Navy, was designed for detecting larger ships and warships, not small wooden fishing boats. The secondary radar, a commercial Furuno system positioned atop the sail, could detect smaller vessels. Both the officer of the deck and the lookout had access to the information it provided.

As the lookout peered into the darkness, unable to discern potential dangers, he took it upon himself to check the secondary radar, even though it was not in his formal job description. When he saw a blip on the radar screen, he alerted the officer of the deck. Although they could have dismissed it as an anomaly, the blip persisted and indicated that they were on a collision course with a small vessel. The *La Jolla* took swift action to avoid disaster and came to a dead stop just thirty yards ahead of an unlit rowboat containing two fishermen. Without the lookout's diligence and inquisitive mindset, a catastrophe would have occurred.

Afraid to Speak

A questioning attitude in healthcare is no less important than in the nuclear navy. Without it, disasters happen. Unfortunately, questioning circumstances beyond one's scope of responsibility isn't a practice that has been encouraged in healthcare as it has been in the nuclear navy. In fact, such a questioning attitude may be interpreted negatively as impertinence, or even insubordination, and punished accordingly. This problem afflicts not only healthcare but also most types of institutions.

A story is told about Soviet Premier Nikita Khrushchev, who was visiting the United States after the death of infamous dictator Joseph Stalin. Khrushchev sat in a room jam-packed with reporters. One reporter called out, "Mr. Khrushchev, can you tell us why you didn't speak up to challenge the horrible things Stalin was doing?"

Khrushchev glared at everyone in the room, slammed his hand on the table, and demanded, "WHO SAID THAT?" The room went deathly silent. Khrushchev pounded the table again and yelled, even louder, "I said, **WHO SAID THAT?**"

Not one reporter made a peep. None of them even dared to twitch. Khrushchev slipped back in his chair, smiled, and said calmly, "*That's* why I didn't say anything."[94]

A Questioning Attitude in Healthcare

One study found that more than 50 percent of nurses had felt unsafe speaking up about an issue that could have negatively affected patient care. Twenty percent of nurses reported that they experienced this type of situation a few times a month. The nurses were more likely to tell their supervising manager about the danger than to confront the practitioner making the mistake. But fewer than half of the managers followed through and reported the safety issue.[95]

In conversations about their hesitancy, most nurses our safety team spoke to admitted that they had sometimes remained silent when they noticed a problem at work.

"Why didn't you speak up?" we'd ask.

Some would answer, "I didn't think it was my place to question the doctor." Others would say, "I didn't want to get my head bitten off like I did last time."

Another common reason given was that they were unsure what "right" looked like. That is, they suspected that something was wrong with the procedure, but they didn't have enough knowledge or confidence in their level of understanding to express their misgivings.

A final deterrent often mentioned was not knowing the correct time or place to speak up. Should they say something during the procedure or afterward? Should they wait to be asked?

When leaders and safety team members have these kinds of conversations with staff, they dispel the myth that asking questions is somehow inappropriate and reinforce the importance of a questioning attitude. They can remind individuals at all levels that feedback is valued, and each person should feel psychologically safe to speak up. The organization must also ensure that its staff understands procedures well enough that they *do* know what "right" looks like and can feel confident speaking up.

A Missing Sponge

An incident occurred at one hospital a while back that perfectly illustrates the importance of a questioning attitude.

At the end of a procedure, before the surgeon closed up the patient, his team inventoried the tools and supplies used during the operation and assured the surgeon they were all accounted for. However, when the team did a recount of the items after the surgery was complete—but before the patient was moved to recovery—they found that one sponge was missing.

"The count isn't right," the surgical tech said.

The surgeon had already left the room. When he was found and told of the issue, he returned, fuming, and demanded, "What do you mean, the fucking count's not right? You told me . . ."

"I'm sorry," the tech replied. "We made a mistake. We checked the trash, we checked everywhere, and we can't find the sponge. We think it must still be in the body."

"I *know* it's not in the body!" the surgeon bellowed, even though the only logical conclusion was that it was. "Just move the patient out," he ordered.

If a surgical team moves a patient out and then later must bring the patient back to the operating space, that's considered a sentinel event—a code 15 in Florida—and it must be reported to the state healthcare agency. If the patient remains in the operating room, however, the team can open up the body again without triggering a code 15. The procedure isn't finished until the operation is completed.

The tech courageously replied to the surgeon, "You may be right, but I'm going to order an X-ray to be safe. We're going to verify that the sponge is not still in the body."

"Fine, do what you have to do," the surgeon snapped, "but you're wasting my time."

The team had an X-ray taken, but since none of them were radiologists, they couldn't positively identify the sponge inside the body. And so, the tech went one step further. "Listen," he said, "I don't know if this shadow on the X-ray is what we think it is, but I'm going to have an X-ray taken just of a sponge, to see what it looks like." They did so and found the two images matched.

The surgeon reluctantly reopened the body and, sure enough, found the missing sponge. He grabbed it and threw it across the room, spattering blood everywhere, then stormed out.

Despite the pressure from the surgeon, the tech had a questioning attitude that day. The tech's actions and perseverance were extraordinary. Although he didn't know for certain that a sponge had been left inside the patient, he understood the grave repercussions—especially for the patient—if such were the case.

Along with a questioning attitude, the tech exhibited integrity, formality, and a higher level of understanding. The surgeon, on the other hand, failed to uphold any of these standards, and his surly behavior made the situation more difficult for all.

Everyone in an HRO, regardless of their position, needs to have a questioning attitude. In practice, this amounts to the democratization of safety. Every employee must be able to say, "I have a voice, and I am listened to. I'm part of a team that cares about me. I can speak up and, together with my team, fix things." Adherence to this fourth pillar alone can improve the culture of an organization.

Creating a Culture of Professionalism

Unlike the surgeon in the above story, a true leader and genuine professional never attacks those who have questions. They are not threatened by suggestions or another pair of eyes watching their process. Indeed, a professional realizes that this type of backup from their team will only serve to make them better and improve safety and outcomes for their patient.

A professional leader not only accepts feedback—they ask for it. They communicate openly with their staff and tell them, "If you see something wrong, tell me. I need your help."

Physicians who encourage their team members to speak up consistently have better safety records and boast lower complication rates than others.[96] When people believe their leader cares for them, they'll risk voicing their concerns.

The combined IQ of a room will always far exceed the intelligence and experience of any single individual, regardless of talent. And at some point, we all make mistakes—we're human, after all. A sleepless night, an argument with a spouse, a moment of distraction . . . all could lead an experienced clinician to miss something or make a mistake doing a procedure they've done a thousand times before. When that time comes, we all desperately need our coworkers to have our backs. When we are distracted, we need individuals in the room who are willing to say, "Doctor, I believe you skipped a step," or "The count wasn't right. We need to find the missing sponge."

Some healthcare organizations now have a center for advocacy or a professionalism committee focused on ensuring a high degree of medical professionalism. When a physician becomes disrespectful, abusive, or otherwise inappropriate, an anti-professionalism claim gets submitted. Someone from the monitoring center or committee may first discuss the matter with the offending party over coffee. If that encounter brings no acceptable results, the process will escalate. A senior-level executive may speak with the physician next. If the situation does not improve, the case will then go to the med staff for review.

When issues of unprofessionalism are addressed, complication rates go down and patient safety goes up. Intimidating behavior keeps others from asking questions, thus inhibiting high reliability healthcare.

The HIPPO Should Wait

Because many clinicians won't challenge a superior's decision, even if they think it is wrong, we have changed our time-out procedure by having the surgeon speak last. We want to encourage others to share their thoughts, whether or not they coincide with those of the surgeon.

Author and organizational psychologist Adam Grant writes about the drawbacks of the HIPPO (highest paid person's opinion):

> The most dangerous voice in a meeting is the HIPPO . . . Status disparities can fuel conformity and groupthink. When you need diversity of thought, ask everyone else to share their views before turning to the HIPPO.[97]

Stanford professor Bob Sutton also commented that a HIPPO often takes after their namesake with a big mouth and little ears (speaking much and listening little).[98]

There's no doubt that surgeons, executives, and leaders at every level have a great deal of expertise and insight. We are not at all saying that their opinions don't matter. However, a questioning attitude in others does not undermine or minimize a leader's process or knowledge; it enhances it.

The Importance of Psychological Safety

Psychological safety stands out as a prime measure of a thriving organizational culture. When employees perceive that it's safe to express themselves, they will readily do so. They will point out potential safety issues and other areas of concern. They will back up their peers and superiors and offer ideas for improving quality and efficiency.

In the absence of a nurturing and caring environment founded on trust, employees hesitate to voice their concerns. Knowing they will be ignored—or worse, punished—for speaking up, workers shut down. They become apathetic and keep their thoughts to themselves—sometimes with tragic results.

We saw an unfortunate example of this in one particular intensive care unit that used extracorporeal membrane oxygenation (ECMO), a heart bypass system. An ECMO machine may be used with a patient waiting for a heart transplant or someone who suffered a major heart attack, for example. The patient's blood is pumped outside of their body into the heart-lung machine, which removes carbon dioxide and sends oxygen-filled blood back to the tissues in the body.

Since the ECMO machine acts as a substitute heart, it is critical to the life of the patient. The ICU team practiced what they would do if the ECMO machine stopped working. With a second machine on hand, they ran through the proper way to connect the various cords from one machine to the other, quickly and effectively, so the patient's substitute heart would continue to pump blood to their brain.

One afternoon, the machine suddenly did stop. But the physician, the CO of the operating room, had not taken part in the practice exercise. Nevertheless, he said, "I got this. I got this."

When his trained people tried to help him by providing vitals and other information, he shouted, "Stop! Shut up!" and proceeded to incorrectly hook up the second ECMO machine. He took a connection that should have gone to the return and hooked it up to a dead end, producing no flow. The tech watching him knew the surgeon was doing it incorrectly.

While the physician floundered, blood had stopped flowing to the patient's brain.

After the incident, a safety team member questioned the tech: "Did you know the surgeon was hooking up the machine incorrectly?"

The tech's hands began to shake. "Yes," she replied.

"Then why didn't you say something?"

"I didn't want to get screamed at again," she said. "And he ordered me to shut up."

The surgeon created a psychologically unsafe environment for the nurse and the rest of his team. They didn't feel loved, trusted, or even free to speak up. By discouraging backup from his team, the physician put his patient's life at risk.

12

BACKUP

The fifth pillar of high reliability is "backup." This means that if you see a problem, own it. Stated simply, team members have one another's backs. They keep an eye out for each other and step in to help when they see an issue, even though it's not *their* problem.

A questioning attitude and backup overlap and intersect. A questioning attitude may be more about challenging procedures and asking yourself if everything is as it should be, while backup relates to the way you extend yourself for others.

Backup is monitoring and assisting in work that isn't strictly your responsibility. It goes beyond the call of duty in order to strengthen one's team. In part, backup means speaking up even when it's more comfortable to remain silent.

For the pillar of backup to work, team members must trust one another and care for each other. Why would someone provide backup for another person if they knew they would receive only grief and trouble in return? Backup functions best when all team members know that everyone has a deep commitment to securing the welfare and success of every other person on the team. This understanding stems from a healthy culture and a positive leader. People are more inclined to support someone within an organization who genuinely cares for them.

Backup in the Nuclear Navy

During an Operational Reactor Safeguards Exam (ORSE), a vital external examination that gauges a ship's capability to operate safely, the crew on the USS *Texas* was tasked with demonstrating their ability to deal with a critical steam leak. The submarine conducted a drill wherein the reactor was intentionally shut down while submerged at sea. This involved the insertion of all control rods to initiate a reactor shutdown, commonly referred to as a SCRAM. In the course of this procedure, materials engineered to absorb neutrons were introduced into the reactor core, effectively ceasing the critical nuclear reaction.

Subsequently, the crew had to isolate the simulated steam leak, then raise the control rods back into position, and finally restore the reactor to a critical state, all while being closely monitored and timed. This exercise involved four key participants in the maneuvering area: the electrical operator, responsible for electrical plant operations; the reactor operator, overseeing all reactor plant operations; the throttleman, in charge of the throttles and the steam plant; and the engineering officer, who supervised the entire operation.

One of the primary objectives of the exercise was to assess the crew members' proficiency in utilizing the "box," a small room measuring about four feet square located in the engine room. This room could be pressurized in the event of a steam line rupture, providing a safe space for sailors to coordinate necessary repairs and control the reactor while shielding them from harm. Since the space was isolated, backup was limited to a small group of watchstanders.

Outside the box in the engineering spaces, the sailors addressed the simulated steam leak and subsequently received the order to initiate the reactor startup procedure. The reactor operator had a specific sequence to follow within a tight timeframe. Speed was crucial since a significant amount of stored energy had been lost. He reviewed his checklist, which included the critical item of setting a switch from "scram" to "normal" on his panel. Correct positioning of this switch was essential for the control rods to engage and enable the reactor to start. This task was just one of a dozen that required swift execution.

For some reason, however, he missed the step.

Fortunately, the electrical officer, whose responsibilities were completed by that point in the drill, continued to pay attention as the reactor operator worked through his tasks. Just as the reactor operator said, "Switch lineup complete," the electrical officer interrupted him, shouting, "Stop! Your scram switch isn't in the normal position."

The reactor operator said, "Oh," and went through the whole process again, this time moving the scram switch to normal.

That is an example of backup. The electrical operator watched what the other members of his team were doing, noticed something was not right, and spoke up, even though he had no obligation to confirm this switch lineup was correct.

By ensuring that a single switch was in the correct position before the scram breakers were shut to commence the startup, the electrical officer prevented a significant delay in restoring the reactor and a considerable decrease in performance during the examination. His assistance not only resolved the issue but also boosted the ship's reputation and grade on the exam. The display of teamwork greatly overshadowed the reactor operator's isolated mistake.

Backup in Healthcare

Backup in healthcare can take many forms. It can be a physician's effort to get another physician the information they need promptly, for example. If an emergency medicine physician orders an X-ray to be taken, *stat*, the radiologist who reads the image shouldn't merely submit a report and hope that the emergency doctor will see it at some point—especially if the image indicates a significant problem. The radiologist must stop what they're doing and contact the attending physician immediately.

Backup can mean having a second set of eyes. Colonoscopies are performed one of two ways: by an optical scope (a physician looks through a scope as it traverses the patient's colon) or by CT scan (a patient ingests a contrast that lights up the walls of the colon). In the latter case, a radiologist reads the scan, backed up by another radiologist or computer-assisted read. The backup reduces the number of small polyps missed from rare to zero.

Many hospitalized patients have leads on the chest and torso that monitor every beat of their heart and electrical rhythm. The nurse assigned to the patient is trained to pay attention to the monitor and act on alerts. The monitor is engineered to notify the nurse of any abnormalities. In addition, unit staff often watch another set of monitors on the nurse's station. Monitor techs working from a remote monitoring station also focus solely on a select group of patients. All of this is backup in action.

Backup can also mean having an assist, or a second set of hands. Finding a good vein to start an IV isn't always easy. Yet, there's usually one nurse in each unit that seems to have a preternatural ability to start an IV on any patient—sometimes with the aid of a handheld ultrasound. That nurse's willingness to use their talent and help out when others are struggling is a prime example of backup.

A Routine Procedure Gone Bad

When fifty-nine-year-old Joe visited the emergency room, seeking help for severe leg pain, the physician on call told him, "Joe, you have a blood clot, but try not to worry. This is a routine procedure. We'll give you heparin—a blood thinner—and then we'll remove your blood clot. After that, you should be good to go. No problem at all."

Though it *is* a routine procedure, administering heparin can be quite dangerous because it thins the blood. If a patient has any bleeds, especially in the brain, it could be fatal. To prevent this, the nurse giving the drug must first do neuro checks by asking the patient simple questions: "Who's the president of the United States? What year is it? What year were you born?" The neuro checks can reveal if the patient has any cognitive issues.

If everything seems fine, staffers can start administering a heparin drip, which starts the blood-thinning process.

The accepted heparin protocol calls for neuro checks at the beginning of the procedure, then every two hours thereafter. At the six-hour mark, workers are required to take a blood draw and send it to the lab. A partial thromboplastin time (PTT) test measures the time it takes for blood to make a clot. Blood that is too thin can increase a patient's chances of significant bleeding. Any reading beyond 100 or 125 indicates the nurse should immediately stop the heparin drip and call the doctor.

In Joe's case, an inexperienced nurse failed to do the initial neuro check, and she took the sample at the three-hour mark instead of the six-hour mark. When she realized her mistake, the nurse disregarded the lab results, even though the PTT was already dangerously beyond the normal range—over 200 seconds.

Her action displayed both a failure to follow protocol and a failure of understanding. The lab results indicated that Joe's blood thinning far exceeded the requirement, and he was in extreme danger. She should have stopped the heparin drip and called the doctor immediately. The nurse didn't comprehend the meaning of the results, however, and so failed to act.

Eventually, Joe started to vomit. They rushed him to the emergency room, where he died of a brain hemorrhage.

Had the nurse followed protocol, Joe's death could have been prevented. If the nurse had received more training on properly administering the drug, Joe's death could have been prevented. If the nurse had had backup . . . *Joe's death could have been prevented!*

For the well-being of our patients and staff, we must fully equip our caregivers with tools rooted in the five pillars of high reliability before they are thrust into life-or-death scenarios. All five pillars were ignored in this instance, and you can observe the consequences.

Despite these examples, healthcare does not systematically encourage the practice of backup in many areas. Too often, there's a "stay in your lane" mentality, or the feeling that "I don't need to speak up if something doesn't affect me directly."

We need to move to a culture of vigilance. If you see it, own it.

Each day, nurses catch something that physicians missed, or techs notice something that nurses didn't see. Every single professional, at all levels in healthcare, needs to back each other up. This extra level of vigilance should never be interpreted as a negative. It is simply a double-check—a seatbelt, a safety harness, a backup parachute. It's the type of fail-safe every high-stakes industry needs. Imagine if RaDonda Vaught had had that kind of backup.

A Quick Review

Like Admiral Rickover, leaders wanting to turn their companies into HROs need to start with the right culture. When employees know they are cared for, valued, and listened to, a culture of trust is created that will form the bedrock of a high reliability organization.

The next step is setting clear, high standards and instilling them into all workers to the extent that they become second nature throughout the organization. The five pillars are cultural expectations of high reliability:

- A higher level of understanding—having both a deep knowledge base, particularly related to one's duties, as well as a broad understanding of purpose
- Integrity—exhibiting personal integrity by doing the right thing no matter the circumstance, and organizational integrity by providing staff the full support they require
- Formality—respecting rules, following communication protocols and procedures, and avoiding work-arounds
- A questioning attitude—challenging things that don't look right, seeking better ways, and being a critical thinker

- Backup—looking out for others on the team, watching their processes, letting them know if they've missed something, and helping out when needed

As the stories we've told illustrate, the five pillars intertwine and build off one another. When a safety issue occurs, its root cause usually comes down to a failure of not one, but multiple pillars. Conversely, a pattern of great outcomes and safety scores is a telling indicator that most—if not all—of the five pillars are hard at work in an organization.

While these foundational elements of leadership and expected standards are large contributors to the nuclear navy's remarkable safety record, additional layers of defense lie in behaviors and system processes designed to enhance reliability.

In Part Four, we'll compare the fortifying behaviors and system processes of the nuclear navy to those in healthcare, and look at similarities, gaps, and opportunities for improvement in the following areas:

1. Certification standards
2. Proactive mindset
3. Transparency
4. Accountability and safety structure
5. Sustainment

The effectiveness of any tool used by an HRO hinges on well-defined behaviors and expectations such as these, as well as the underlying rationale behind their implementation. Let's get started.

PART FOUR

BEHAVIORS AND SYSTEM PROCESSES

13

CERTIFICATION STANDARDS

Jens Rasmussen, a human factors and safety expert, researched various industries, looking for what prompts individuals to make mistakes. He found that the causes of errors primarily fall into one of two categories, knowledge based or distraction based, depending on the level of experience of the individual performing the task.[99] Understanding which type of cause is at the root of an error is critical for addressing the error appropriately. Blanket answers won't fix every problem.

Ahead, we'll discuss apparent cause analysis, our simple, yet effective way of identifying the root cause of an error. We'll also look at distraction-based errors and ways to combat them, but because of the tremendous reduction on knowledge-based errors the right approach can have, we want to begin this chapter focused on training and credentialing.

The Novice

We've all been the novice at some point—new and unskilled, doing the best we can but messing up anyway. The truth of this shared experience was made evident by a swell of heartwarming and hilarious "dear intern" stories shared online after an intern at HBO mistakenly sent out a test email to all subscribers. In response to HBO's explanation and apology of the mishap on Twitter, hundreds of people wrote back to encourage the intern and share their own humiliating blunders. Here are two of our favorites:

> Dear Intern,
>
> When I was 25, I made a PDF assigning each employee to the Muppet they reminded me of most. I meant to send it to my work friend, but I accidentally sent it to the entire company. My supervisor (Beaker) wanted to fire me, but the owners (Bert & Ernie) intervened. –Aerin

> Dear Intern,
>
> One time, I sent out an email on behalf of the organization's Board of Directors with a link to a custom thank you video that was meant to show appreciation. The link redirected to a lady in her pajamas loudly reviewing Hot Cheetos recipe fails. I cried twice that day. –BCP[100]

The groundswell of support for the intern was heartwarming, and the sharing of embarrassing stories went on and on. But in a high-risk industry, errors are not a laughing matter.

We know "intern mistakes" are bound to happen. Research shows that novices have a 50 percent chance of making an error the first, second, or third time they perform a task. Think about the implications of that. That's like flipping a coin with patient safety. The question is, what to do about it?

Making the novice feel supported and acknowledging that it's easy to make errors when one is new are good ways to make them feel psychologically safe. It's also important to ensure them of backup and teach them that asking questions when they have doubts is not just a nice idea, it's a requirement.

Like the nuclear navy, healthcare must formalize the expectation that novices and experienced employees alike face every task with a questioning attitude.

Training

It's also critical to ensure that a novice has the training needed to do their job. The nuclear navy is acutely aware of the error rate associated with inexperienced personnel, and as a result, its certification processes are demanding, especially the qualification procedures. Recently qualified nuclear-trained officers are required to spend numerous hours on watches, where they are closely monitored while on duty. They must perform supervised watches in all areas, not just their specialized field. This allows them to gain a comprehensive understanding of the entire engine room operation.

Moreover, all nuclear sailors must meet proficiency requirements. For instance, if a sailor hasn't performed a specific watch within a specified timeframe for any reason, they are disqualified from that watch until they undergo a formal upgrade, which includes interviews, to ensure their continued proficiency.

These stringent standards are significantly more robust than the current requirements in healthcare. In nursing schools, for example, prerequisites vary. Some schools fail to offer essential hands-on training. Because of this, there are new nurses who may lack proficiency in common tasks, such as managing blood sugar levels, inserting catheters, or interpreting fetal heart monitor readings. They may never encounter a real-life critical patient until their first day on the job, at which point they might be asked to administer care without direct supervision.

Imagine this scenario: A nurse straight out of nursing school has passed his RN certification and just finished a twelve-week training program for the emergency department. One day, he finds himself on his own in the emergency department with a few patients assigned to him. A patient comes in who is diabetic and suffering a hyperglycemic, life-threatening event. The doctor orders fluids and insulin. Unlike the old days, when plastic bags were hung on a drip stand, IV fluids are now generally dispensed using a twenty-first-century pump.

So, the nurse must hook up the medication and the fluids. He has given this medication before, but he has never trained on this pump.

Although the task requires high attention, his low familiarity with it may confuse or distract him, reducing his focus, which means he has a 50 percent chance of making a mistake. What will happen?

If the new nurse has a questioning attitude, he will find a veteran nurse to ask for help, and a mistake may be averted.

But a high reliability organization wouldn't just encourage a questioning attitude. An HRO would have been proactive, providing the nurse with training on the pump beforehand and ensuring that he was monitored the first several times he was required to use it.

Too often, the person making the error is made to bear the full brunt of responsibility. But considering the learning curve a new worker has to overcome, this is hardly fair.

Recredentialing

Novices aren't the only ones making knowledge-based errors. Experienced clinicians make them too when their skills become rusty.

A surgeon who takes out a prostate must get recredentialed every three years. But the recredentialing process isn't extensive—just some continuing education classes and a few cases. This refresher may be sufficient for those surgeons who perform a thousand prostate surgeries annually, but it's certainly not enough for the surgeons who only do five in a year.

How do we judge a surgeon's skill? Though complication rate data is often referenced, it is unreliable because of incomplete reporting and, therefore, of little use. However, there is a good way to test a surgeon's skill that some healthcare systems do employ. Surgeries that are performed robotically are recorded through the lens of a viewing system. Surgeons in some organizations must submit ten or so cases per year to get blind-reviewed by an expert, who will grade the surgeon on technique, efficiency, bleeding control, and other parameters. If the surgeon receives a score in the top quartile, that's great. If the score is average, the surgeon is encouraged to polish their weaker areas. If the score falls below a certain standard, however, the surgeon is not allowed to do the procedure until they can demonstrate that they've improved and achieved the technical proficiency required.

Unfortunately, there are no state or federal laws mandating this kind of testing currently. But it makes a lot of sense, doesn't it? Who would want a surgeon who fell into the lowest category operating on their loved one?

The question brings to mind a recent TV ad for a cellphone company that opens with a nervous patient lying in a hospital bed with his concerned wife sitting next to him in a chair. A nurse inspecting a chart stands on the other side of the bed.

"Have you ever worked for Dr. Frances?" the wife asks the nurse.

"Oh, yeah," the nurse replies. "He's okay."

The worried patient asks, "Just 'okay'?"

The camera moves to the doorway of the hospital room, where we see a doctor about to enter. The physician says happily to a person offscreen, "Guess who just got reinstated?"

He walks into the room and says to himself, "Well, not officially."

Then the physician approaches his anxious patient and says, "Nervous?"

"Yeah," the man replies with some force.

"Yeah, me, too," the doctor replies, but with a dismissive wave of his hand, he continues, "Don't worry about it. We'll figure it out."

He then turns his back to his clearly horrified patient, starts to walk out of the room, and says, "I'll see you in there."[101]

The ad makes a good point. No one wants an "okay" surgeon. If we required robust recredentialing and skills assessments, no one would have to settle for one.

When Training Gets Canceled

Certainly, healthcare doesn't need to emulate the nuclear navy precisely, but it should incorporate more rigorous training, mentoring, and ongoing proficiency processes. The up-front investments in time and money undeniably save lives, which should be the paramount objective. Moreover, they enhance productivity, reduce litigation expenses, and generate long-term cost savings that far surpass the initial investment in an enhanced certification process.

Unfortunately, many organizations forgo these long-term benefits in lieu of short-term costs savings. The following tale of a canceled skills fair illustrates this shortsightedness.

The maternity wards throughout one healthcare system held periodic skills fairs to provide up-to-date, hands-on training for their nurses, ensuring the nurses' skills stayed fresh and relevant. Unfortunately, the COVID-19 pandemic made it necessary to cancel in-person training.

The skills fair was found to be more effective than computer-based training, so after the pandemic was over, preparations for an in-person skills fair began.

These fairs require significant effort from both the organizers and attendees. Educators must plan and practice their material, and nurses must coordinate their work schedules and make the personal arrangements necessary to attend. Nevertheless, the majority of nurses enthusiastically welcomed the return of the skills fair. They were deeply committed to their patients and saw the value in training to enhance their critical skills.

The nurses of one maternity ward in particular were especially eager for the skills fair. Their ward had experienced three infant fatalities in a single year due to medical mistakes. They had a new director but no manager in place, and they had been grappling with various safety issues resulting from inexperienced nurses and a high influx of traveling nurses. Several physicians had expressed their concerns about the ward's safety. The timing for the skills fair couldn't have been more crucial.

However, on the evening before it was to occur, the skills fair was abruptly canceled. All of the meticulous planning and effort that went into the event went to waste. Both the patients' needs and the staff's eagerness to meet those needs were disregarded.

The cancellation was solely driven by financial considerations, though the hospital system had a higher profit margin than most healthcare systems. Each of its campus CEOs were judged by their units' productivity rates.

And if fifty nurses were to attend the skills fair in the same pay period, the productivity rate would dip below the company's 100 percent target rate. So, the CEO decided to cancel the training and simply hope there wouldn't be another adverse event.

The negative impact this decision had on safety is obvious, but imagine how it influenced the organizational culture. How did the nurses—who had eagerly signed up for the training, recognized the urgent need for it, and adjusted their schedules to attend—feel when they received a last-minute notification about the fair's cancellation? Did they have faith in their organization's explanation of budget constraints when the system's profitability was common knowledge? Obviously not.

With one poor last-minute decision, the hospital's leader undermined the nurses' trust and the culture of the organization, by failing to uphold the values of organizational integrity and neglecting to prioritize a higher level of understanding.

Eliminating Distractions

While ongoing training is critical, it isn't going to fix every sort of problem. Returning to Rasmussen's study, let's explore the other main cause of errors: distractions. Seasoned workers don't commit errors because they are unfamiliar with their tasks; instead, their errors often stem from distractions of various types—frequent interruptions, a sleepless night, insufficient training of support staff, or interpersonal issues with colleagues. Such intrusions contribute to the veteran worker's frustration and divert their focus.

Consider this example: A seasoned general surgeon who has done a few thousand appendectomies makes a mistake during a routine appendectomy. Maybe they don't tie off a bleeder, or they nick something during surgery. It's an error that they rarely, if ever, make. They have high familiarity with the task and complete knowledge of how it should go, but they were on autopilot when they made the mistake. They had argued with their spouse the night before and hadn't slept well as a result.

The surgeon does not need a remedial course on appendectomies. Such a review would be a waste of time and entirely miss the cause of the surgeon's error.

As Rasmussen suggests, the hospital system must correctly identify the root of an error in order to address it correctly. To accomplish this, our healthcare system employs a tool called "apparent cause analysis" (ACA) with the five pillars of high reliability incorporated into the process.

Apparent Cause Analysis

For decades, the standard in the healthcare industry for analyzing the cause of a negative event was a "root cause analysis" (RCA^2). In the past ten years, the National Patient Safety Foundation developed guidelines and processes to help make the review more action-oriented and renamed it "root cause analysis squared" (RCA^2) to reflect the improved focus.[102] Both are formal ways to address a mistake and take weeks or even months to complete.

To speed this slow-moving procedure, we took a lesson from the nuclear navy and streamlined it. The new process, apparent cause analysis, uses a simple two-page form with checklists and open-ended questions. Safety officers begin by describing the event and naming the level of harm it caused. They go on to recount the immediate and remedial action taken. Next, safety officers must evaluate twenty-one actions or competencies related to the five pillars and decide if each was met (such as "knew and understood standard operating procedures" and "adequate supervisor and/or precursor oversight"). The safety officer next must list the contributing factors they identified, and they must write an apparent cause statement, their description of what "right" should have been, and how what transpired deviated from "right."

This pared-down version of RCA^2 takes hours rather than weeks or months and pinpoints perhaps 90 percent of root causes, allowing us to quickly implement both short- and long-term corrective actions.

Additionally, having the five pillars incorporated into the ACA helps to set behavioral expectations. Communication that references the five pillars becomes natural and part of daily practice.

ACAs are necessary because finding the root cause of issues isn't always easy. Take the underwhelming response to a patient with sepsis symptoms, for instance.

When someone comes into an ED with chest pain or symptoms of stroke, the medical team jumps into action. When a patient presents with signs of sepsis—mental confusion, elevated heart rate, depressed blood pressure, and a raging fever—it rarely garners the same response. But it *should*.

Sepsis is the number one killer in hospitals. Up to half of deaths that occur in healthcare are sepsis related.[103] For every hour treatment of septic shock is delayed, a patient's risk of death increases by 8 percent.[104]

Every clinician knows the dangers of sepsis and the necessity for quick action. The patient's blood must be drawn for lactate testing and blood cultures, appropriate antibiotics must be administered, and plenty of IV fluids must be given. These steps are so vital that CMS requires healthcare facilities to report whether they were completed within the first three hours of a patient's arrival, a period called "time zero."

So, why do we repeatedly see cases where care was delayed? If the need for urgency is clear, what's preventing it?

Perhaps the overemphasis on efficiency metrics is to blame. Emergency rooms track such times as "door to doctor" and "decision to discharge," and appear to be more successful when more patients are treated quickly. This focus might lead a nurse to process five easy cases over a case with a slower treatment process.

Efficiency metrics are important, but wrongly applied, they can lead to trouble.

To get to the root of such a problem, we must refer back to the five pillars. Are we demonstrating organizational integrity by emphasizing patient care over efficiency metrics? Are we adequately staffing and supplying our departments to set our nurses and physicians up for success? Do the clinicians understand the signs of sepsis and know how critical immediate treatment is?

Are they following sepsis protocols? If there is something wrong with the protocol or something keeping them from following it, are they questioning it?

Though there are potentially many contributing factors to various issues like sepsis response, an investigation based on the five pillars helps the safety team filter through them, identify the root cause(s), and design effective corrective actions.

Trending Errors

In addition to helping us find the root cause of individual errors and negative events, ACA helps us to spot failure trends.

If we find that the majority of errors occurring in a department or unit are knowledge based, then we can concentrate our corrective actions on additional training and the certification process. If, on the other hand, we determine the majority of errors are not due to a lack of knowledge, we must focus on the environment and pinpoint the overarching source(s) of distraction. Problems might range from over-tasked workers to difficult, angst-inducing supervisors. Sometimes the solution is obvious—hire more staff, coach the supervisor—sometimes it takes a bit of applied creativity and exploration of culture issues.

The following story illustrates how our analysis helped us pinpoint the underlying cause of one nurse's errors and creatively and effectively resolve the issue.

The Red Apron Solution

Part of the duties of one very experienced nurse was to assign correct medications to the various patients on her floor. It was something she knew how to do and had always done very well. But at some point, she started making many errors.

Initially, the clinical executive team discussed requiring the nurse to complete remedial training courses. However, the safety leader said, "First, let me conduct an observation and watch her work routine."

As the safety leader watched the nurse, they saw how integral she was to everything happening on the floor. She worked behind a main station and prepared medications at certain times of the day. As they continued to observe, however, they realized that regardless of when she sorted medications, many nurses, doctors, and technicians would continue to come up to her to ask questions—and that's when she made the errors.

So, what kind of remediation would be appropriate? Certainly not a refresher class! Someone came up with the idea of giving the harried nurse a red apron to put on whenever she handled the medications. The apron would send the message, "I'm busy now and can't be distracted. Please hold your questions for later." This highly skilled nurse didn't need additional training; she needed a way to avoid distraction. The red apron solved the problem so well that a similar solution was adopted in many units throughout our system. With a red line, we designate a particular space as a medication counting area. When a nurse stands behind the line, no one should talk to them. It's a simple but effective way to minimize distraction-based medication errors.

So Long as Humans Are Involved . . .

So long as people deliver healthcare, mistakes will be a fact of life. But the research and insights of Rasmussen will help us to better understand mistakes. Tools such as ACA can help us to identify whether the root cause of an error is due to distractions or a lack of knowledge and address it in a specific and highly effective way.

To achieve genuine high reliability within an organization, it is imperative to establish a strong connection between culture, the foundational five pillars, and behavioral and systemic processes. All three components are indispensable for significantly lowering the likelihood of errors and enhancing patient safety.

In the upcoming chapter, we will discover that becoming a high-reliability organization also entails the crucial practice of foreseeing challenges and taking proactive steps to address safety concerns.

14

A PROACTIVE VS. REACTIVE MINDSET

Effectively managing safety requires two spaces: safety one and safety two. Safety one is reactive; issues get addressed after they happen. Safety two is proactive; potential problems are identified and planned for. Spending the majority of time in the safety two space is obviously preferable. That's the norm in the nuclear navy.

Fighting Fires

Functioning in a safety one space is much like putting out fires. It's difficult, stressful, and gritty work. The stakes are a lot higher in safety one, and the energy required to cure an issue is twenty times more than the energy needed to prevent it.

Safety two is anticipatory and periodic. It is a fire marshal writing procedures, updating building codes, and checking exit pathways. It allows time to think critically, compare options, and make unrushed decisions.

In healthcare, we seem to be spending most of our time putting out open flames. There's no time left to investigate wisps of smoke, let alone establish new safety protocols.

We really need fire prevention in healthcare. Do we have smoke detectors? If so, do we regularly change their batteries? Are our systems fire resistant?

When we anticipate what could go wrong and build appropriate responses, we will greatly decrease the major errors that lead to devastating firestorms.

The Problem Pyramid

The Naval Nuclear Propulsion Program (NNPP) uses a pyramidal approach to addressing problems, focusing on third-order deficiencies (see diagram).

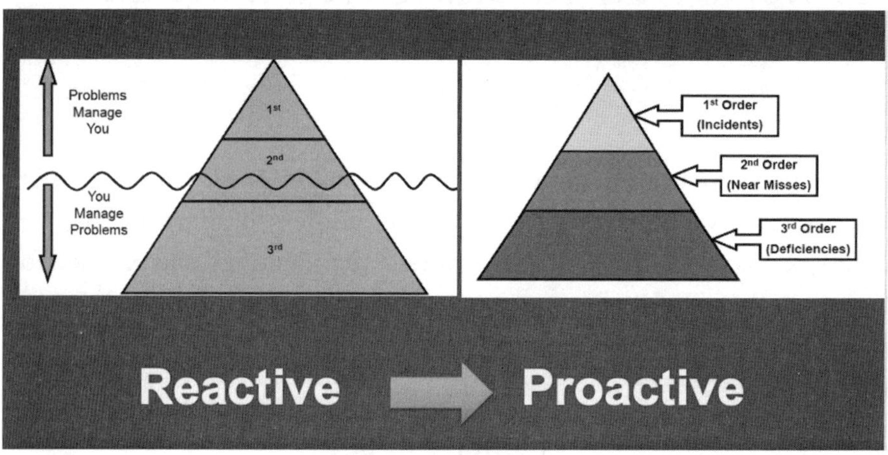

Sailors handle small, third-order deficiencies, such as maintenance and supply needs, before they become problems. They don't work around them, they address them.

The second order concerns near misses that had the potential to become dangerous but got caught before anything seriously bad happened. The navy strives to minimize such occurrences. Ahead, we'll discuss how the navy celebrates each near miss, works to find its root cause, and puts measures in place to ensure it doesn't happen again.

The top level of the pyramid involves incidents where harm does occur—first-order deficiencies. Harmful incidents are more likely to happen the more often an organization tolerates the daily existence of third-order deficiencies.

The NNPP triangle illustrates that addressing third-order deficiencies will directly reduce the number of more serious issues. When a work environment is filled with incidents and near misses, the organization is not controlling its problems; the problems are controlling the organization.

In healthcare, "never events" like a wrong-site surgery or a preventable death are at the tip of the pyramid. The fallout from them consumes enormous amounts of work and time, and the events must get reported to the state.

Second-order deficiencies, or near misses, occur regularly in healthcare. An example of this would be if a wrong dose of medication was given to a patient, but the mistake didn't cause significant ill effects.

We experience third-order deficiencies in healthcare every day. Maybe there's too much clutter in a space, or a patient that didn't get fed or discharged on time. Sloppy, casual care is probably 99 percent of the problem. We're so busy with the tip of the pyramid—with all of our systems focused on the top—that 99 percent of third-order deficiencies often go unaddressed.

The Broken Windows Theory

If fixing third- and second-order deficiencies helps to minimize first-order deficiencies, what happens when these smaller, seemingly insignificant problems are left unaddressed? As you might imagine, the answer is not good.

In a 1982 article for *The Atlantic*, George Kelling and James Wilson outlined their "broken windows" theory, which they formed based on the earlier experiments of psychologist Philip Zimbardo. Kelling and Wilson's theory holds that communities refusing to fix their broken windows lack the ability to build communal pride or cohesion. Substandard environments communicate negative messages to both residents and outsiders. Criminals see all the broken windows and assume that those in the community either cannot or will not defend themselves from unlawful activity, thereby making themselves and their neighborhood easy marks. Broken windows symbolize a community's vulnerability and powerlessness and imply the residents will not stand up for one another. By contrast, communities that stick together fix their broken windows, demonstrating that they intend to assert control over their neighborhoods.[105] Because of this, Kelling and Wilson suggested that police departments should spend more time focused on preventing small crimes and misdemeanors.

With murder rates in New York City at an all-time high in the early 1990s, the city's mayor was ready to put the theory to the test. The police began by preventing individuals from jumping subway turnstile lanes. They then focused on such crimes as graffiti, public marijuana use, and the sale of loose cigarettes. As arrests for misdemeanors increased, murder rates decreased dramatically. Fixing the small-order deficiencies produced the sense that New York City was vigilant and tough on crime—a sense that greatly deterred more serious crimes.

A 2001 study of crime trends in New York City showed that rates of both petty and serious crime fell significantly after these policies were implemented. Even better, crime continued to decline for the following decade. Though critics suggested that other factors may have played a role in the dropping crime rates in New York City, the follow-up research Kelling conducted with colleague William Sousa convinced him that policies based on the broken windows theory did in fact reduce crime and increase community livability in the city.[106]

In the nuclear navy, if someone finds a broken window, they mend it. The nuclear navy prevents catastrophic events—saving lives, time, and money—by consistently managing small-order deficiencies.

The same should be true in healthcare. Yet, when we ask a person in charge of risk if they have time to look at second- or third-order deficiencies, they often answer that they are in crisis mode and only have time to address "never" events.

It's not easy to switch to prevention mode when flames are actively burning. But an organization must allocate personnel and resources to do just that. Not only do little, unaddressed problems send a negative psychological message to an organization's employees and patients, they can line up at times, creating the possibility for a catastrophic event to slip through the breakdowns or holes in safety.

Beware of Swiss Cheese

The same small-order deficiencies that served as broken windows in Kelling and Wilson's theory are the dangerous holes that align and allow for disaster in James Reason's "Swiss cheese" model. Reason's aptly named model compares safety systems to layers of Swiss cheese. According to Reason, multiple layers of safety systems will ensure an error-free outcome, unless each of those layers has a hole—a vulnerability—and the series of holes allows the error to pass through all the safety measures unchecked.[107] The explosion of the space shuttle *Challenger* was a tragic example of the Swiss cheese model in action.

Just seventy-three seconds into its infamous 1986 flight, the *Challenger* blew up 46,000 feet over the Atlantic Ocean, killing all seven aboard. To this day, most Americans believe the disaster was caused by a frozen O-ring. That's what we were told at first, after all. The truth was more complicated. A series of small-order deficiencies went uncorrected and lined up perfectly to cause the catastrophe.[108] The O-ring was just the final hole in the last layer of cheese.

The 2010 disaster on the oil rig *Deepwater Horizon* is another real-life example of the dangers that occur when problems remain unaddressed and holes in safety align. The British Petroleum oil rig caught fire, exploded, killed eleven people, and wreaked tremendous ecological damage along the Gulf Coast.

The Big Fix, a 2012 documentary about the event and the causes that led to it, concluded that the rig's operators were so driven by financial considerations that they didn't attend to small-order deficiencies. They cut corners and addressed only what they had to address to keep the rig going. They completely ignored safety two issues. The catastrophe killed eleven people and untold numbers of animal life, spewed 134 million gallons of oil, and led to the largest environmental damage settlement in US history—$20.8 billion.[109]

The day before the explosion, in the height of irony, several BP managers flew to the rig and celebrated the crew's record of seven years without an injury.[110] But the streak was due to dumb luck rather than rigorous maintenance, training, and safety procedures. And, unfortunately, luck is not a plan. It cannot be depended upon.

A better strategy that is far more dependable—though possibly less exciting—than relying on luck is simply addressing small problems with consistency before they grow into large ones. Focus on safety two, mend broken windows, and fill the holes in the cheese. We've illustrated the benefit of taking proactive measures toward safety with these different concepts to highlight its importance.

Celebrating Near Misses

Perhaps you are wondering how a healthcare organization can stay attuned to small-order deficiencies and incorporate the five pillars into day-to-day practice? One way may seem counterintuitive, but not when viewed in the proper light. Celebrating near misses is about transparently acknowledging a problem, learning from it, and expressing gratitude that it didn't cause significant harm.

The nuclear navy celebrates near misses so that they don't happen again. Healthcare does not celebrate them, for two primary reasons. First, many healthcare organizations don't have the safety staff needed to effectively manage a program that recognizes near misses. And second, hospitals are *extremely* careful about what they report to the state and regulating agencies, or share between campuses and other hospital systems, because of the possibility of multimillion-dollar lawsuits.

Celebrating near misses bleeds over into the category of "transparency and sharing lessons learned," which we will discuss in the next chapter. We will give examples of why transparency is important despite the legal risks and show how a lack of transparency can have far worse repercussions on culture and the bottom line.

But first, we'll look at ways we've found to celebrate near misses within our healthcare system.

Speak up for Safety (SUFS)

To increase the reporting of safety issues, we began celebrating those who alerted us to the problems.

The safety representatives from each campus in our region would meet monthly and describe the issues that had been reported to them. Then, the safety committee would rate the severity of each problem and celebrate the catch accordingly. If someone reported a problem that could potentially have fatal consequences, for instance, that employee with the questioning attitude would receive a gift, recognition from the CEO, and an article in the organization's newsletter.

The reports from the monthly meetings would then be reviewed by the safety committee. If any of the problems that were reported had significant consequences and could affect many campuses, the information would be taken to the corporate level and disseminated system-wide.

The more celebration these issues received, the more additional concerns were brought forward by others—which was definitely a good thing. People wanted to be a part of making the hospital safer. And who doesn't want to be celebrated? SUFSs created the psychological safety workers needed to speak up.

Shortly after we started SUFSs, the number of reports we received increased exponentially. This phenomenon tracked with the results of a recent study that found that, as an organization's reporting goes up, its adverse claims go down.[111]

The Importance of the Five Pillars

As we use tools like SUFSs and ACAs, we continually refer back to the five pillars to see where the breakdown in safety occurred. We have found that the root cause of any safety issue can always be traced to a failure to keep one or more of the pillars.

Not only do we document all the ACAs and SUFSs, but we also track the cumulative data we receive to identify trends. Are we repeatedly failing in a particular pillar more often than the others? Is the level of severity in errors connected more to any one pillar? Which pillar makes the greatest impact on safety?

By returning again and again to the five pillars, we raise the level of standards accepted within our organization, and so change the culture. Too often, the culture of an organization doesn't place a high value on following procedures. Employees may treat procedures they don't like the same way people treat strange, outdated laws that have gotten left on the books—by ignoring them. (Did you know it's illegal to skateboard in Florida without a license? It's also illegal for unmarried women to parachute on Sundays!)[112] Of course, useless, ineffective procedures should be questioned and eliminated, but the practice of ignoring standards and procedures is a safety hazard and needs to be rooted out.

Shortly after new needles with flip-top safety caps were introduced on one of our campuses, a nurse manager in the emergency department admitted to us that he didn't use them. Though the needles were safer for both the patient and the provider, they required an extra step that the old-style needles did not. The nurse manager preferred the faster, familiar needles, and so hoarded what was left in inventory.

The nurse manager's actions revealed a departure from the five pillars on many levels, especially in formality and personal integrity. They also showed the organization had failed in integrity by introducing a new tool and procedure without validating or monitoring it.

When workers ignore the procedures they don't like, there's a culture in need of change. ACAs and SUFSs are helping us to do exactly that.

Safety Stand-Down

When too many second-order deficiencies are occurring in the nuclear navy, we use a tool to reset standards and shock the system called a safety stand-down.

Some years ago, one of our hospitals had a concerning number of wrong-site surgeries. The chief medical officer (CMO) and the chief nursing officer (CNO) were at a loss as to what to do.

"In the navy," we told them, "if you get to the point where you're performing below standards and experiencing excessive drift, you create a moment of shock. A ship immediately stops doing what it's doing, discusses what happened, reviews the standards, and then resets behavior."

We used this example: On one mission, Bob began to see many unaddressed small-order deficiencies, indicating to him that the ship's standards were not being met. For example, the ship was late providing a steam generator sample, and some periodic maintenance wasn't getting done. Once he recognized the uptick in complacency and drift, he pulled his submarine off station and stopped its mission. He took a whole day to talk to his crew about standards and to reset their work habits.

The hospital followed the navy's example and instituted safety stand-downs. Now, after a significant mistake, everyone talks together about what happened, discusses what standards were missed, and then resets in order to move forward.

We also standardized time-out procedures before surgery. Before a patient receives anesthesia, the surgeon takes a time-out with the patient and surgical team to ensure that everyone is on the same page. This simple, safety two formality is a powerful proactive safety tool.

A Continual Effort

A lot goes into managing safety, but it's largely about tackling small issues before they become big ones. And while there are many tools to help you develop a safety two focus—such as ACAs and SUFSs, stand-downs and time-outs, testing, and training—it's not always easy. Yet the continual effort and push toward safety impacts culture and makes a world of difference.

Bruce Grooms, whom we highlighted in our discussion on leadership and culture (see chapter six) was Bob's commanding officer on the USS *Asheville* and one of his most influential leaders. Grooms would routinely say, "It's not what happens to you, but what you do to ensure it doesn't happen again."

He understood that he couldn't foresee every adverse or near-miss situation, but he could take charge of corrective actions and address minor issues as a leader to ensure the safety and well-being of everyone under his command. He recognized that safeguarding the crew depended on addressing these smaller issues. Because his sailors saw how Grooms genuinely cared for them and worked to keep them safe, they reciprocated that affection. The result was a remarkably healthy culture and amazing success.

In the upcoming chapter, we will discuss the crucial behavioral practices of transparency ("calling the baby ugly") and sharing lessons learned.

15

TRANSPARENCY

Organizational transparency is openly sharing information about a company's operations with the aim of establishing clarity, trust, and accountability among its stakeholders.

In the nuclear navy, the personnel involved in a near miss or an incident resulting in harm promptly share relevant information with the entire fleet, celebrating the lesson. This practice serves several purposes: to prevent future occurrences of similar issues, enable others to learn from their mistakes, and nurture a culture of trust.

Though the nuclear navy has never had a radiological incident in over 6,200 reactor years, non-nuclear mistakes have certainly happened on occasion.[113] When they do, they are managed with transparency so that others may learn from what occurred. A perfect example of this involved a ship that had an incident with an open interior hatch.

When a submarine gets underway, it uses a formal process called "rig for dive." Each compartment of the sub follows a detailed procedure to make sure that every valve and switch is lined up appropriately. The crew must ensure watertight integrity and check that all systems are functional, so that if the ship needs to surface in an emergency, it's ready to go.

A petty officer must sign a logbook to certify that rig for dive was completed in their assigned space. Then, a second officer must check each of the compartments and independently verify that everything was done properly. The last compartment to be checked is the bridge, or the sail. It is made watertight with redundant hatches—an upper hatch fitted to the top of the submarine, and a lower hatch providing a secondary seal.

As commodore, Bob once got a call from a concerned mother who told him that an incident had occurred on her son's ship; the lower hatch had been left open. The oversight hadn't caused any damage in the case because the upper hatch was closed, but if the sub had suffered an accident, they could have lost the ship. Water would have entered the people space at a rate that couldn't be controlled.

Fully informed of the issue, Bob openly admitted the mistake to the parent and shared what had been done to prevent future recurrences. Though no catastrophe had actually taken place, the CO of the sub in question had treated the open hatch as a major problem, conducted a root cause analysis of the error, and taken immediate and long-term corrective action.

Despite the possibility of looking bad, the CO had reported the incident to his base commander and to others in his squadron. Within a week, every submarine in the fleet knew about the incident, why it had occurred, and how to prevent it themselves.

This transparent behavior for the benefit of others is deeply embedded in the culture of the nuclear navy and an almost automatic response. Unfortunately, we can't say the same thing about healthcare.

The Urge to Hide

In healthcare, the urge to hide near misses is hard to overcome. Fear of reprimand, job loss, reputation damage, and even lawsuits may keep workers quiet when a mistake has been made. But unshared lessons can't be learned, and a lack of transparency will lead to far greater costs in the long run—top among them, lives that could have been saved.

Several years ago, a patient opened a hospital window and jumped out. The fatality not only caused terrible grief for the man's family but also triggered a state investigation and, not long afterward, a civil lawsuit.

The incident highlighted the danger of having patient rooms with windows that unlock and open from the inside, but the hospital involved failed to share the lesson learned to other campuses within its healthcare system. A few years later, in a sister facility, another patient repeated the same fatal act through another unsecured window. Again, the healthcare organization was taken to court. Because it had known about the problem and hadn't fixed it system-wide, the financial penalty increased exponentially.

Had the hospital implemented effective measures to tackle the problem and openly shared the incident's details for the benefit of both their own system and others, it could have enhanced safety across the country, and a tremendous amount of grief could have been prevented. However, the safety lessons were kept hidden. The hospital favored the risk of another incident at a different facility over the legal risk of being transparent. This kind of backward thinking is driven by the leaders of an organization and is far too prevalent throughout healthcare.

Shifting Blame

We were summoned to address serious safety concerns at a small rural hospital facility where there were reports of deeply ingrained cultural issues that appeared to be linked to a high number of safety problems. After gathering some information, we requested a meeting with the campus CEO. Our primary intention was to offer assistance and gain a better understanding of the situation.

During the meeting, we began discussing the list of the safety allegations made against the facility. Each time an issue was raised, the CEO's response consistently shifted blame away from the facility and onto the employees. For instance, when an employee named Jim reported concerns about safety storage issues that could directly impact patient care if a patient coded, the CEO countered by mentioning that Jim was currently under an HR action plan for poor performance, essentially discrediting Jim's claim.

The pattern continued. Each time an issue was introduced, the CEO found fault with the person raising it.

The pivotal moment came when we brought up a problem that had been thoroughly verified. Unlike the previous cases, where the allegations were based on independent interviews without verification, this incident involved the hospital shutting off oxygen to the ICU patients due to contracted maintenance. Many safety protocols were neglected or bypassed, such as briefing the clinical team before the maintenance was performed, having a backup oxygen supply readily available, and meticulously inspecting and verifying the piping flow path to ensure it wouldn't affect patients.

Fortunately, quick action by the nurses prevented any harm, but the potential consequences were grave. But when we confronted the CEO, emphasizing how narrowly a catastrophic incident had been avoided, he never took responsibility. Instead, he responded by saying, "What concerns me most is that word of this incident was shared off the campus." He also criticized his CNO for notifying the system CNO of the event. It became all too evident to us that the CEO was not attempting to safeguard the hospital's patients or frontline workers. He was only serving his own interests and reputation.

The leader of an HRO would've managed the incident very differently. First, they would have investigated why the error occurred, then shared the mistake with other campuses to ensure such an error wouldn't happen again. Lastly, they would have celebrated the quick-thinking nurses publicly. This last part would have raised morale, enhanced organizational trust, and strengthened the culture.

We Made a Mistake

Some people may worry that owning up to a mistake will harm their company's reputation, but in fact, the opposite is often true. Remember the HBO intern who sent out the test email to customers (our performance failure example in chapter 13)? HBO could have pretended it never happened and hoped no one noticed. Instead, HBO tweeted:

> We mistakenly sent out an empty test email to a portion of our HBO Max mailing list this evening. We apologize for the inconvenience, and as the jokes pile in, yes, it was the intern. No, really. And we're helping them through it.[114]

Over 5,000 people commented (most of them positively), 21,000 reposted the tweet, and 146,000 people liked it.[115] The intern's mistake turned into a huge publicity boon for HBO.

One commenter wrote:

> This is a masterclass in empathy and transparency and I have 10x more respect for @hbomax now because of it.—Pete[116]

Making mistakes is not ideal, but it *is* expected. "To err is human," after all. What people don't expect are organizations that are open about their mistakes. Such transparency builds trust relationships with a company's customers as well as its employees.

Practicing Transparency

Teaching workers to overcome self-protective instincts by revealing their mistakes is easier said than done, as safety advocate Joann Ankoviak came to realize. Ankoviak, a CNO in our healthcare system, led out in daily safety huddles specifically designed to foster transparency and the sharing of lessons learned. Prior to a safety huddle, Ankoviak learned of a dangerous event that had occurred at one of our hospital campuses. A mentally unstable patient had opened the oxygen valve mounted on the wall in his hospital room and had set the oxygen that flowed out on fire. Thankfully, a caregiver had noticed and gotten the oxygen turned off before an explosion happened. The unit then took security measures to ensure a similar issue could not reoccur.

Ankoviak expected the nurse manager of the affected unit to discuss what had happened in the safety huddle, yet the nurse manager remained silent. Ankoviak spoke with the nurse manager afterward. Despite knowing the purpose of the safety huddles was to share lessons learned, the nurse manager said she had remained silent because she didn't want to air her unit's dirty laundry. The nurse manager had to be reassured that she would not only be safe in sharing it, but that she would also be celebrated for her transparency and insight. The nurse manager shared the story at the very next huddle.

The transparency and culture that Ankoviak fosters has made her a beloved leader and one of the best safety advocates we have worked with.

Effective Ways to Share

Transparency relies on communication, and communication can be enhanced through a variety of tools. One simple tool that our organization has employed for over twenty years is SBAR (situation, background, assessment, recommendation) reporting, also called "results and recommendations." SBAR was introduced to healthcare by Doug Bonacum, another veteran of the nuclear navy, who later became a national patient safety leader with Kaiser-Permanente healthcare system. Bonacum says the need for a concise, organized method of communication came to him when he was sitting in a patient safety meeting with doctors and nurses who were "talking at" each other. The nurses felt the doctors didn't listen to their recommendations; the doctors felt the nurses rambled and didn't make clear proposals.[117]

By using the SBAR checklist, both the doctors and nurses can now know what to expect and can communicate more effectively.

Speak Up for Safety and apparent cause analysis, more recent additions to our communication toolbox, allow us to share discoveries more broadly across our system. SUFSs and ACAs are reported or used almost daily and collected by the safety officer at each of our campuses. Once a month, this team meets in person, with each member discussing their most significant SUFS and ACA reports, then voting on the most pressing submissions.

The team member whose submission gets chosen provides a brief presentation at the monthly Quality, Risk, and Safety (QRS) monthly collaboration meeting. The member presenting provides recommendations on corrective actions, and others in the meeting share their thoughts and experiences. At the end of the meeting, participants define action items and select the appropriate department or leaders to address the issue. Since team members are embedded in different campuses, they return to their own C-suite leaders and share the lessons learned from these submissions.

These lattice structure meetings occur once a month. All lower-level meetings feed into the bigger audience meetings. The patient safety meetings give content to the QRS collaboration, which then feeds into the system-wide safety meeting.

To illustrate how this system works, let's revisit our earlier story about hospital beds shifting from kilograms to pounds.

Because of an incorrect weight calculation, a patient in the emergency department received the wrong dosage of medication. Though metric weights are the universal measure for determining dosage, the scales on the beds in the ED had been set to pounds.

Whenever a safety incident like this occurs, the person involved must report on it to the risk manager, who then must forward it to the nurse manager. Unfortunately, the focus of these managers can be consumed by the necessary paperwork and closing the case versus disseminating information about the problem. Even if the manager does perform safety huddles to inform those on their floor about the issue, there used to be no way for them to pass the lesson on to other departments and campuses throughout the system.

When our safety officer received a report of the bed scale incident, she went to the unit to perform an apparent cause analysis. In her investigation, she discovered that four of the unit's eleven beds were still measuring weight in pounds. Using the ACA form to aid her, the safety officer soon noticed deficiencies in several pillars.

She found that the administering nurse lacked a higher level of understanding because she did not know that she should use kilograms instead of pounds. She hadn't followed standard operating procedure to measure the patient's weight, which meant she lacked formality. There was also a lack of integrity—either from the nurse, for failing to look up the proper procedure, or from the organization for not ensuring the nurse had the proper training. When the measured weight seemed off, the nurse lacked a questioning attitude to find out why. Finally, the nurse received no backup from her nurse manager or engineering, the latter of whom should have caught the problem during audit rounds.

After these discoveries, the safety officer brought her findings to a monthly safety meeting. She also spoke with both the engineering department and the vendor. Eventually, the officer discovered that changing the batteries on the bed automatically reset the bed's scales to pounds. We'd set up our frontline personnel for failure . . . and didn't even know it. The safety officer also discovered an even bigger problem involving bed intake: No one had checked these beds, and no one had any idea how many of these improperly calibrated beds we had or where they all were. The safety officer's investigation revealed *so* many broken windows on this one issue alone.

She then put out the word to ED leaders to share this problem with their teams in their safety huddles. She also informed the C-suite and presented an ACA and its findings at a monthly collaboration meeting, where it was recommended that the information get shared at the corporate monthly performance and safety meeting with 245 safety members across the system. In one stroke, *all* the campuses learned of the problem!

Before ACAs, awareness of this issue would have remained in this single ED, and no one would have even informed engineering. Depending on the busyness of the staff, the bed issue might not have been addressed at all. Our new structure allowed the system to broadcast the problem and its solution across fifty hospitals, thus avoiding future medication errors and dire consequences.

A Dashboard for Barcode Medication Administration

Nowadays, grocery stores have barcode stickers on everything, even on individual pieces of fruit. Barcoding simplifies pricing at supermarkets, but it saves lives in healthcare by helping to prevent medication errors.

Each year, the Leapfrog Group—which bills itself as "the nation's premier advocate for transparency in health care"—grades and publicizes the safety of the thousands of hospitals across the nation.[118]

Barcode medication administration is one of the twenty-seven performance measures that the Leapfrog Group uses to indicate how well hospitals protect their patients from harm.

Because barcoding is so important, we created a business intelligence dashboard to process all the data related to medication administration. By comparing the medication a nurse manually enters into the medication administration record to the medications given and barcoded on, the dashboard compiles data on barcode medication administration rates for hospitals, floors, and even individual nurses.

The dashboard makes barcoding habits transparent and helps us to spot and address areas of concern. If a unit's barcoding rate is less than 80 percent, we take notice. At one point, we learned from the dashboard that one floor's barcoding rate had dropped to nearly 20 percent, so we went in person to the unit to investigate. After speaking with caregivers, we learned there was a simple explanation. The automatic dispensing cabinet was inconveniently placed; in order to barcode, the nurses had to walk a hundred yards out of their way. The solution was obvious: we moved the ADC.

Without the dashboard keeping track and alerting us to poor barcoding statistics, we might have missed this concerning but easily solvable problem. This is a prime example of how sharing information with safety officers can significantly enhance patient safety.

Calling the Baby Ugly

"Calling the baby ugly" may sound a little coarse, but then, military jargon often is. Obviously, it has nothing to do with literally insulting the look of a newborn—we are *not* advising that—but rather, it's a reminder to abandon pretense and denial, and admit to obvious problems. If something doesn't look right, call it out. There's no pretending that all is well when errors or performance outcomes indicate otherwise. Problems are addressed even when doing so is uncomfortable or difficult.

A good example of this happened on one of the ships of Squadron 7 while Bob was commodore. Certain chemicals are used on a nuclear submarine to maintain the chemistry of the steam generator. When the CO of the sub in question was signing a requisition form, he noted that his ship was ordering far more chemicals than was typical. The captain soon learned why. The petty officer in charge of inventory hadn't been keeping careful track. After months of guessing at numbers, rather than actually counting the stock, the petty officer discovered that the ship's inventory had gotten dangerously low on needed chemicals. Instead of owning up to the situation born of his shoddy work, he put in an order to replenish the stock and hoped no one would question it.

Though the inventory would be brought up to appropriate levels before something occurred, something bad *could* have happened. The submarine had been in a risky situation. The ship seemed to have an "ugly baby." Though the CO suspected the problem was isolated to one lazy petty officer, he knew a full root-cause evaluation should be conducted. Unfortunately, the submarine was due for its annual operational reactor safeguard exam (ORSE), an in-depth, three-day evaluation performed by regulatory officers while the ship is underway. The CO shared the issue of the inventory shortfall with Bob and confessed that he was tempted to skip a root-cause investigation for the moment because he had so many other things to do in preparation for the ORSE.

Appreciating the CO's candor, Bob told the captain that getting to the root cause of ugly babies shouldn't be put off. To allow the CO to look into the inventory issue fully and ensure the safety of his ship, Bob gave the submarine extra time by postponing the ORSE.

The CO in this case was quick to admit to the problem on his ship, because the nuclear navy preaches the importance of doing so. When the ORSE was finally taken, the ship passed it successfully. The decision to postpone the ORSE to allow time for a root-cause investigation was not only essential for setting a positive precedent, but it also had the potential to uncover more significant cultural issues that might have gone unnoticed otherwise.

Systemically Ugly Babies

Not every mistake is an ugly baby. Sometimes an error is just an error. An ugly baby is something much bigger. It's a pattern of errors with a root cause. It's systemic. It's the smoke that alerts you to the fire.

Healthcare is filled with ugly babies. If you'd like some examples—don't worry, we've got plenty, beginning with an infusion center that was brought to our attention for a myriad of problems.

Infusion centers are places where individuals with cancer and other immuno-compromising diseases go to receive medications intravenously. Certain places within these centers—such as the rooms where medicinal compounds are mixed—*must* be kept sterile. To ensure this, inspectors visit each infusion center monthly to swab surfaces, test air quality, and determine whether the amount of particulate present in the sterile areas falls within the appropriate bounds.

After the infusion center in question failed six monthly inspections in a row, our safety team was notified. Our root cause analysis found the major contributors to contamination were basic: how workers washed their hands, covered their beards, and so forth. We also found dirty equipment strewn about everywhere, creating many places for spores to hide and grow.

When we spoke with the workers of the center, the reason for their apathy and sloppiness became clear. They were discouraged. Their facility consistently ranked in the last percentile of infusion units across the system. Their manager was a poor leader who lacked understanding and left a host of issues unaddressed. To the workers, there just didn't seem to be any point in trying.

Sometimes areas in healthcare resist calling the baby ugly for fear of looking bad or getting in trouble or in a short-sighted attempt to avoid costs. In this case, the ugly baby was rooted in a poor leader and a culture poisoned by apathy. Whatever the cause of an issue, we know that acknowledging an ugly baby is the first step to fixing it.

An Unfortunate Response

One hospital had three significant close calls in a row involving three different doctors who nearly operated on the wrong site during an orthopedic procedure.

Some safety staff got on the phone with the COO and the CMO. The safety members told the leaders, "We have a problem. It's only a matter of time until we have a wrong-site surgery." They knew they needed to get to the root cause, look at the culture, the expectations, the standards. Having three near misses in a row clearly indicated they had a big issue that needed immediate attention.

Unfortunately, the COO responded by stopping the safety person mid-sentence and saying, "Listen, I just want to make something perfectly clear. We did *not* have a wrong-site surgery. And I don't want to make this a big deal."

What motivated the COO to say this?

First, Florida is one of the most litigious states in the country. If an incident like this ever went to court—if it were discovered that those executives knew they had a problem and didn't fix it—they would be held responsible. For this reason, a leader might avoid acknowledging a problem for as long as possible.

Second, a lot of organizations and campuses are under significant financial pressure. They're already lean as it is, and if they need to fix something not in the budget, another area will suffer. Workers may choose not to report certain safety concerns for fear of diverting funds from projects higher on their priority list. Unfortunately, safety issues left unaddressed will cause significant harm, sooner or later.

This instinct to deny problems also has a negative impact on culture. According to research cited by the *Harvard Business Review*, "92% of employees said they would trust their senior leader more if that leader would be more transparent about their mistakes."[119] The report also found that the number one reason people want to work for an organization is trusted leadership. We've given examples of poor leaders who have passed blame around and denied there was a problem. The cultures that existed in those situations were some of the worst we've ever seen. By contrast, there was Ankoviak, a transparent leader who shared problems with the sole purpose of solving them and caring for the team members she served. Her team culture was amazing, and her team's results were equally so.

Ankoviak realized that every organization has ugly babies; it's nothing to be ashamed of. To the contrary, spotlighting problems helps achieve solutions. Being transparent with what we know helps us fix issues faster and ultimately saves team members from liability and becoming secondary victims. If someone knows about some problem but does nothing before an incident occurs, then they're culpable in the incident.

We need to call it like it is. If it's ugly, we need to call it ugly.

Even if it's our own baby.

16

ACCOUNTABILITY AND SAFETY STRUCTURE

Accountability is aligning words with actions; it's fulfilling responsibilities. The importance of accountability in the healthcare sector cannot be overstated. Employees seek it out and demand it. When it is missing within an organization, team members disconnect and become apathetic about work. When accountability is present, on the other hand, employees stay engaged and attentive, which significantly improves patient safety.

Once again, the nuclear navy offers a helpful model. It has representatives from an autonomous regulatory entity called Naval Reactors embedded on bases, squadrons, and ships. These representatives do not report to base commanders, commodores, or captains, however. They answer to the independent body of Naval Reactors. This structural arrangement preserves accountability while preventing undue influence from operational leaders and has been successfully implemented by other major organizations such as Disney.

The importance of an independent safety board was made devastatingly clear by the *Columbia* space shuttle disaster. The *Columbia* Accident Investigation Board found that NASA's current organization does not provide effective checks and balances and lacks an independent safety program.[120]

Despite lessons like the *Columbia,* our government, responsible for safeguarding its citizens, does not mandate an autonomous safety program in all hospitals and care facilities. Currently, the Joint Commission only requires one individual per hospital license to be accountable for performing specified risk reduction activities and threat interventions.[121] This is an inadequate answer to the shocking statistics of harm we see in healthcare every day.

Nevertheless, for the benefit of their patients, institutions must do better by going beyond the minimum requirements and establishing a robust, independent safety structure.

Independent Safety Structure

Psychologist and author Henry Cloud spoke at a leadership conference in May 2022 about lattices and roses. If you want to build a beautiful rose garden, Cloud pointed out, you need a structure to support its growth. If you plant a hundred roses and have no structural plan—no lattice to guide them—the roses will remain straggly and never achieve remarkable growth. But if you build a lattice structure—something the roses can climb on—over time, you'll get a beautiful garden with rose-covered walls and arches. A lattice structure allows individual pieces to work together to create a better whole.

This type of safety structure—this accountable, transparent, cooperative culture—would benefit healthcare just as it does the nuclear navy. Not only would it allow for valuable information to be shared and put to practical use by others in the organization, it would make such accountability and sharing automatic.

Cloud asked, "Why do you brush your teeth when you wake up and before you go to bed? Because it's a habit, a structure." We must make critical practices habitual throughout healthcare. We must incorporate them into our structure so everyone in our organization is rooted in them and grows stronger because of them, as happened in the case of the incorrectly set bed scales that we shared in the previous chapter.

Because our safety team had a newly constructed lattice structure in place that supported the quick and widespread sharing of critical information, the information about the beds was easily communicated across the system. Without it, none of this knowledge would've been disseminated. It confirmed for us the necessity of having the right structure in place.

We have seen remarkable results throughout our hospital system as we have learned to leverage our safety structure to become more accountable. Campuses learn from one another, and procedures have become more standardized.

Reporting has also increased because employees expect their concerns will be addressed. This is especially significant because research shows that when hospital staff report more incidents, litigation claims against the hospital drop.[122]

Once you have a culture of accountability and a lattice structure to address safety concerns, you will move significantly closer to becoming an HRO.

Leaders of such an organization must not only be honest with others, but they must also be honest with themselves. They can't avoid confronting embarrassing or problematic realities. They must address them head-on and realize that it may hurt at first, but in the long run, it will benefit the organization, the employees, and, most importantly, the patients.

Where Does the Buck Stop?

"Passing the buck"—a phrase first used in the game of poker—has come to be synonymous with blame shifting. But President Harry S. Truman was not a fan of shirking responsibility. Wanting to emphasize his personal responsibility for the actions of his administration, Truman popularized the phrase "The buck stops here." In fact, he had it written on a plaque that he kept on his desk.[123]

Our question is, where in healthcare does the buck stop? In the nuclear navy, each person believes the buck stops with them. From the engineering technician to the leading petty officer to the commanding officer, each person claims responsibility for the issues that arise. Every sailor claims the buck.

The same should be true in healthcare. The nurse in triage, the medical assistant taking vitals, the tech starting the IV, the physician doing the initial evaluation—every single person in the line of care must believe "the buck stops with me." Responsibility—and blame—can't be left to the CEO alone; the sooner issues are addressed, the better.

In a speech delivered at Columbia University in 1982, Admiral Rickover succinctly outlined his management philosophy:

> A major flaw in our system of government, and even in industry, is the latitude allowed to do less than is necessary. Too often officials are willing to accept and adapt to situations they know to be wrong. The tendency is to downplay problems instead of actively trying to correct them. Recognizing this, many subordinates give up, contain their views within themselves, and wait for others to take action. When this happens, the manager is deprived of the experience and ideas of subordinates who generally are more knowledgeable than he in their particular areas.[124]

Companies known for their customer service, such as USAA, Viking, Disney, and Publix, don't have employees who do less than necessary. Rather, they each empower their personnel to solve the problems they encounter . . . to own the buck . . . to call out and address ugly babies. For healthcare to become highly reliable, this kind of team effort and mentality shift is critical.

The Crucial Role of the Safety Team

It's easy to confuse a safety team with a risk management team, but the two entities are very different. One of the risk team's purposes is to protect the organization from litigation. Because risk management has the authority to report an employee to the state, jeopardizing that individual's license, workers who have made a mistake are naturally hesitant to share that information with the risk team.

The safety team must operate as "priests," building relationships and trust within units, allowing employees to report confidentially and without fear of jeopardizing their license. Safety officers are not primarily tasked with safeguarding the hospital's reputation or finances, though their efforts may have positive effects on both of these. Their main focus is ensuring the well-being of the hospital's patients and staff by promoting a culture of safety.

During the infancy of our new safety structure, we had a PET lab that was riddled with safety concerns. We planned to do conversational rounds in the unit with the imaging safety officer, Karina Coapstick, and we invited the safety officer embedded in that campus to join us. The campus safety officer, who showed up with a checklist, immediately started peppering the intake staff member with questions and demanding documentation of procedures. It was off-putting, to say the least.

We quickly interrupted, explaining that's not what we do. We moved on to a PET technician, described ourselves as safety priests, and established a rapport with her. We asked her for her top three concerns. It was like putting a quarter in a jukebox; all sorts of complaints came out like a song. It allowed our safety team to identify areas of focus—areas that would never have been uncovered with a checklist. We learned there were cultural shortcomings in the unit. Many decisions made by the department's leader made workers feel like commodities.

Once we were able to identify and address the issues, the PET lab team felt cared for, and the safety practices, as well as the culture within the lab, greatly improved. It was a win-win.

Those Who Do Not Learn from History

In healthcare, a harm event triggers an RCA^2. Though "high reliability" has been a buzz term for years, an RCA^2 doesn't typically reference any principles of high reliability. But when we conduct an RCA^2, we now incorporate the five pillars.

Several years ago, before our safety team and reporting structure were in place, a tragic incident occurred that *should* have led to immediate change in safety procedures. A patient who had taken drugs was left unmonitored on a gurney in an ED as she waited for treatment. She coded and no one knew, so no one came to help. The young woman died in the hallway. The incident triggered a full six-week RCA^2 analysis. Countless firefighting hours were expended by clinical leadership and the risk team to address the issue.

Unfortunately, the risk person at the first hospital didn't communicate the problem to other hospitals in the system, and the RCA^2 didn't result in any new safety processes—at least, none that were sustained. The lack of an effective way to disseminate lessons learned meant that history was doomed to repeat itself. Two years later, another hospital in our system had an almost identical situation. A patient came in with chest pains, wasn't monitored, and died.

This time, the regulator imposed an immediate jeopardy citation, which could have caused the hospital serious financial repercussions if the safety concern had not been promptly resolved. The hospital, including its top-level executives, mobilized extensive efforts in response to the crisis.

Seeing such effort expended on safety one is frustrating. Such a situation could have been avoided—with much less effort—through prevention, sharing of lessons learned, and the implementation of a sustainable plan.

At about the same time that the immediate jeopardy order was issued, a third incident occurred at yet another hospital in the system. Fortunately, this one was a near miss with no fatality. An elderly patient was admitted to the ED and indicated he had chest pain, yet was left unmonitored.

When the campus's safety officer learned of the event, they sprang into action and conducted a proactive apparent cause analysis. With this quick and effective investigation that takes a few hours rather than the weeks needed for the RCA^2, the safety officer soon uncovered several issues.

First, they discovered that the ED used only a three-step telemetry checklist versus the more rigorous five-step checklist that other EDs within the system employed. Second, they learned the provider assigned to the patient was a traveling nurse who worked for multiple healthcare systems in various regions and didn't know the three-step telemetry protocol for properly monitoring ED patients.

The safety officer also noted that no one assisted the nurse or checked to make sure their patients were being monitored. Four of the five pillars had been violated: higher level of understanding, organizational integrity, formality, and backup.

To prevent such incidents from recurring, we examined the telemetry protocols for each facility and instituted the more rigorous five-step process in each ED. We also shored up training for new and temporary employees and strengthened verification procedures.

If we hadn't had the lattice structure for sharing information and the safety structure for conducting the review, this proactive approach could have never happened.

Permanent Fix vs. Whac-A-Mole

Sometimes the problems in a process can feel never-ending. One error is discovered, workers implement a fix, and then another error occurs in a different part of the process. It can feel a lot like a game of Whac-A-Mole.

Take the biopsy process, for example. A biopsy sample follows a complex and intricate trail through a healthcare system. In the operating room, a sample of tissue gets removed and placed into a specimen cup. The cup is labeled with patient-identifying details and transported to a histology lab, where it is prepared appropriately, often on slides, for a pathologist to view through a microscope.

All aspects of the process—ordering, transporting, preparing, and reading of results—must be performed meticulously, without mix-up or break in the chain of custody of the specimen, but occasionally an error will occur.

We need a proactive approach for anticipating problems. One way to do this is by having the safety team perform a failure mode and effects analysis (FMEA). The FMEA was developed by reliability engineers for the military in the 1950s and used by NASA in preparation for the *Apollo* launches.[125] While an RCA[2] is a specific way to analyze problems *after* they occur, FMEA is a structured method of addressing problems beforehand. A good FMEA will gather representatives from all areas involved and comprehensively review the components and subsystems of a process, identify potential failure modes, and suggest preventive actions.

Our systematic conversation-based rounds and the trusted relationships built between frontline workers and the safety team also reduce drift and the Whac-A-Mole problem. By staying in close communication with frontline workers, we can stay alert to small issues before they balloon into large ones.

We can mark our calendars and schedule times, months and years down the road, to discuss important lessons learned and ensure updated processes are being sustained. That way, a newly hired nurse will still benefit from the lessons that predated them. They'll know to double-check that a hospital bed is set to kilograms. They'll know to leave the person measuring medications behind the red line alone. They'll know that patients in the ED must be monitored. The conversations also serve as good reminders for veteran clinicians.

Disseminating information through conversation-based rounding and consistently returning to verify that corrective actions are still in place prevents the natural tendency toward drift. It also helps you win the game of Whac-A-Mole.

Someone to Point To

Who has the responsibility for establishing a safety structure and performing tasks such as FMEAs and ACAs within a healthcare organization? Joint Commission and DNV don't.

If no one is assigned the responsibility of completing safety analyses, sharing lessons learned, and establishing relationships, then those things are simply not going to be done, or at least not in a consistent manner.

Admiral Rickover said, "Responsibility is a unique concept. . . . You may share it with others, but your portion is not diminished. You may delegate it, but it is still with you. . . . If responsibility is rightfully yours, no evasion, or ignorance, or passing the blame can shift the burden to someone else. Unless you can point your finger at the man who is responsible when something goes wrong, then you have never had anyone really responsible."[126]

An organization with an independent safety team, rooted in high reliability, has someone responsible to point to. Someone to hold them accountable. Someone vital to safe patient care.

17

SUSTAINMENT

Years ago, a tragic incident occurred at a hospital where a baby lost its life, prompting the initiation of an RCA^2. The investigation unearthed safety concerns around the administration of the drug Pitocin, and the team determined that moving forward, two healthcare professionals must be present when a mother is given that medication.

Six months later, upon revisiting this RCA^2, it was discovered that the newly established protocol had not been adhered to; there was still a failure to ensure the presence of two individuals during the Pitocin procedure. The initial investigation had merely identified the problem but failed to bring about substantive changes. There was no accountability or sustainment.

This illustrates one of the reasons why we have so many reoccurring harmful events in healthcare. When lessons learned get lost, it's a failure of the system, not the people. You can put all the corrective actions and procedures in place, but if they are not maintained, they do no good at all.

Sustainment is the prevention of drift and the maintenance piece of formality—and something the nuclear navy is particularly good at. Following the example of Admiral Rickover, the nuclear navy builds robust sustainment strategies into its processes and carries them out with consistency.

Right from the outset, newcomers are educated about the unique culture of the nuclear navy, emphasizing the significance of formality as a fundamental cornerstone for long-term sustainability.

Once the navy establishes a corrective action plan, it conducts rigorous rechecks to make sure that the plan has been implemented effectively. It asks knowledge-based questions validated with oral and written exams, and audits maintenance and training logs on a periodic basis with unannounced spot checks. All this ensures that the positive results are maintained.

Though hospitals have quality teams that do audits to prepare for inspections from DNV or Joint Commission, error rate statistics suggest these fixes are mostly temporary. Such preparations are similar to the scramble of getting a messy house in order before company comes over. After the visitors leave, drift inevitably occurs.

We're not suggesting that the quality team isn't important to hospitals, but they can't be the only ones responsible for meeting safety and inspection requirements. To succeed, they need the collaboration of a risk team and a safety team, who bring different approaches and safety tools to the table.

Safety officers revisit past RCA^2 reports, monitor the implementation of corrective actions, engage in conversation-based rounds, and employ a number of other tools to make sure corrective procedures are being sustained. In this chapter, we'll discuss these sustainment strategies and give examples of them in action.

Conversation-Based Rounds

A conversation-based round is a safety tour of a unit or department in which we ask caregivers questions about their processes and concerns, give them the opportunity to identify any barriers to compliance, and offer direct feedback. It's a simple way to identify and fix smaller-order deficiencies, build trust, and improve culture. Such rounding is not a new concept, but unless it's formally instituted, it usually doesn't happen.

In many healthcare organizations, a quality audit generally comes down to a person with a checklist visiting floors to observe employees in action. Without engaging in conversations, however, auditors identify only 10 to 20 percent of the problems that are present. By communicating and developing relationships with those involved, we can discover a great deal more.

Such discoveries are often made when we meet periodically to set goals and identify our greatest opportunities for improvement. When we asked our risk management personnel to identify the most common causes of adverse events, they did some data analysis and returned with an answer: "We have the greatest opportunity with glycemic management and medication errors."

Our statistics were not unusual; medication errors are a problem globally. The World Health Organization says that "unsafe medication practices and medication errors are a leading cause of injury and avoidable harm in health care systems across the world."[127] And the Department of Defense says that "medication errors represent approximately 50 percent of all patient safety events reported by military health care facilities."[128]

We decided to investigate the issue with conversation-based rounds and learned that the nurses were making medication errors because they were failing to barcode. This was attributed to several causes: Sometimes, the Wi-Fi didn't work. Sometimes, the medicine didn't have barcodes. Some medications had too many barcodes (for differing purposes) and caregivers got confused about which one to use. Occasionally, timing was the problem.

Staff were meant to administer certain medications within an hour of the glucose sample, which was taken by an independent contractor.

"My schedule doesn't coordinate well with the person who takes the glucose sample," one caregiver told us. "Yes, I'm required to deliver the medication within one hour of the finger prick, but I don't get here until an hour and ten minutes later. I don't barcode because I'll get dinged when I can't follow the requirement. So, I'd much rather not barcode, give the patient the medication, and hope that they don't get ill."

By delivering the medicine without barcoding, the nurse reduced her apparent rate of noncompliance. Such a practice, though, could have hurt her patient.

We never would have made these discoveries had we relied only on an auditor checking off boxes. Conversation-based rounding creates connection. Through it, we can uncover roadblocks that keep staff from doing their jobs properly.

Just by having conversation-based rounds and doing a couple of simple interventions (such as fixing the Wi-Fi), we reduced our adverse events in glycemic management by half.

Conversation-based rounding on a medical-surgical unit helped us to solve yet another medication issue. Two patient rooms in a single unit shared a refrigerator containing medications. A nurse reached in to get an antibiotic for a patient in room A, but instead grabbed a similar-looking bag meant for another patient in room B—a pre-medication for someone having immunity issues with a transplant. The mix-up caused a complication for the patient and devastated the nurse.

When we discovered the issues with how refrigerator space was divided, our engineering team was able to resolve them. However, if the nurse had remembered to use the barcode on the medication, the mix-up would have been prevented.

Once she realized her error and how it could have been avoided, the nurse became a champion for barcoding. Her advocacy, along with the changes made by the safety team, changed the dynamic of the unit. Personnel started realizing that the organization *wanted* to find and implement effective solutions that would keep both them and their patients safe.

Executive Safety Rounds

Executive safety rounds are a good way to emphasize the importance of high reliability within an organization. When caregivers see that their leaders focused on safety, it encourages them to maintain a safety mindset as well.

Safety rounding is not the same as social rounding. It's not the moment for treats and casual banter. Safety rounding should be a time for executives to notice potential problem areas, discuss the five pillars with frontline workers, and ask open-ended questions like "What can we do to improve the safety or care of your patients?" or "What are your top concerns?" Many leaders will be amazed at the feedback they receive on safety rounds. But the process can't end there!

Problems must be addressed, and follow-up rounding must take place to assure workers they were listened to and that they—and the safety of their patients—are valued by the executives and the organization.

Not every idea is perfect or needs to be implemented, of course, but it makes a big difference to employees just to know they have a voice that gets heard.

When leaders engage with frontline workers, they will discover new, more effective ways of doing things. Successful leaders are not just good at communicating; they're good at listening, and they create psychologically safe environments in which people are encouraged to give feedback and are never embarrassed or reprimanded for what they say.

When leaders round like this, and when they follow up their words with actions, they build trust with their employees. Caregivers will know their input makes a difference, and they will speak up more often.

The safety team can support executives by facilitating their rounds and making sure that their safety findings are addressed, ultimately enhancing sustainability and culture.

Ongoing Training and Testing

Every doctor and nurse gets a certification for basic life support and CPR. Additionally, many physicians and nurses have taken advanced cardiac life support training and know how to restart a patient's heart or get a patient breathing again.

Every two years, practitioners take a two-hour test to certify them in these procedures. Along with the written portion of the exam, the test requires only one hands-on procedure: examinees must place the paddles on the chest of a mannequin, shock it, and then check the pulse. The testing is probably not frequent or rigorous enough for those who may be called upon to do the procedure at any time.

In Chapter 8, we told the story of a patient with an irregular heartbeat, a very common problem. He needed to be cardioverted back to normal sinus rhythm.

The operator said "clear" before he defibrillated but had forgotten to turn the machine to synchronous mode. So instead of sending the patient into normal sinus rhythm, he sent him into ventricular fibrillation, which could have killed him.

The team reacted quickly and was able to save the patient by defibrillating him with five times the normal electrical voltage. Though the patient lived, he had to spend more than a week in the ICU.

This incident happened for two main reasons: 1) the operator hadn't done the procedure in some time, and 2) he was working with a new and unfamiliar piece of equipment.

The event prompted us to make sure that every cardiologist and nurse who works in a cardiac lab throughout our entire healthcare system is not only familiar with the equipment but can also *demonstrate* their skill. Getting "signed off" doesn't mean merely writing a check mark on a piece of paper every few years. It means proving one's proficiency through the regular drills that we've built into the system. The safety team can ensure the sustainment of this crucial process.

Walking the Dog

A patient in one of our facilities died because the hospital lacked a sufficient blood supply to prevent the loss of life in the event of a major bleed. We discovered that it took far too much time to get blood requested and delivered. We knew we needed to fix the process immediately.

So the safety team facilitated a drill. "Pretend this patient needs blood *right now*," we said. "The physician cut the wrong artery and the patient is hemorrhaging. They will die unless you get this person more blood. What do you do?"

We observed their process and discovered that the team didn't know who to call for additional blood, which, of course, delayed getting it there.

We then arranged for blood to be delivered to the facility to see for ourselves how long it would take.

Afterward we critiqued the exercise, looking for opportunities for improvement. We instituted several corrective measures and made sure they would work. Some trials didn't go perfectly, but that was okay—we do drills to improve performance. We were able to take what we learned through the drills at the first hospital to find holes in the processes of sister facilities.

A phrase from the navy called "walking the dog" applies to doing drills. You can talk about walking the dog, and imagine what walking the dog will be like, but you won't really know what you need to know until you actually walk the dog. One of Bob's superiors used to say, "You're not going to carry poop bags until you walk the dog and the dog craps."

Doing drills—walking the dog and validating processes as much as possible—tightens response time, uncovers process issues, and helps teams create more effective fixes. In short, drills help to ensure reliability. They are a necessary part of training and sustainment. But drills alone are not enough. Skills tests are also critical for sustainment.

When we discovered a nurse in one of our labor decks did not know how to do strip monitoring (see Chapter 8), we didn't say, "Here, just watch this video." Rather, we provided complete interactive training and followed it up with an examination. The nurse had to pass a skills test before she could continue to provide care to patients.

Every nurse involved with labor and delivery should be able to read a rhythm strip and put standard nomenclature to it. Every physician who delivers babies also needs to pass a rhythm strip exam. While a few hospitals do require testing for this skill, most do not.

There simply are not enough state-mandated drills and tests in healthcare. To achieve a safety record on par with the nuclear navy's, healthcare must follow the navy's example of conducting comprehensive drills and skills assessments on a regular basis. A robust safety team is needed for this. Part of a safety officer's role is implementing rigorous certification requirements for high-risk skills and ensuring the sustainment of those skills with retraining and recertification at regular intervals.

Organizations cannot become highly reliable by doing the bare minimum mandated by the state—they must do far more.

No News Is NOT Good News

There are some healthcare systems that report, "We haven't had a healthcare-associated infection in 365 days." While such claims sound good, we often are skeptical about them. We wonder if these organizations have such robust procedures in place that they really do eliminate infections, or if they simply report "no infections" because they haven't looked hard enough to find them.

Some healthcare systems lack adequate staffing to properly follow up on cases, which means they send fewer reports to the Centers for Disease Control and Prevention through the National Healthcare Safety Network. Though this type of clean record may look good on paper, it is misleading and fosters a false sense of security. If healthcare systems aren't tracking infections and connecting them to lax safety procedures, standards will continue to drift. Ignorance is bliss until a catastrophe occurs.

If, on the other hand, organizations search for associated infections, they will probably find them. While this won't look as good on paper, a hospital that tracks infections and eliminates their root cause will be able to prevent disasters down the road.

In some cases, misleading "clean" reports aren't just a case of negligence or apathy—they're intentionally written to deceive. The navy calls it "gundecking" when sailors deliberately manipulate reports to hide their failure to follow established procedures (like the petty officer who falsified inventory records in chapter 15). Individuals engaged in gundecking may not see the harm in their actions, but the deceptive practice raises the likelihood of a serious incident.

As commodore of Squadron 7, Bob was responsible for ten nuclear submarines. The commodore of a fleet can't know all the intricate details of what's happening on each boat. They need some way to determine where to triage. They'll always have one or two submarines taking up a lot of their time, some that require just a little attention, and a few that seem to need nothing at all.

When Bob didn't hear anything from one of his subs for a long while, he began to worry. The silence became a beacon to him, letting him know that the sub's leaders weren't addressing their problems. It's not good when reporting drops. Not in the navy, and not in healthcare.

A healthy, robust system reports more events, not fewer. Such a system inevitably finds that the gross number of adverse events goes down over time. That's a successful program. If no one ever complains and no one ever reports an event, it's probably because no one cares or thinks their complaint will make a difference. Or it is because the culture is so bad, everyone is afraid to speak up.

The simplest thing to do about a house in need of repair is . . . nothing. Ignore the clogged gutters, the cracked driveway, and the broken windows. It may be easier, but it's a lousy long-term solution. A high reliability organization must focus on keeping up with ongoing challenges. To do so, it must be aware of them—and that requires robust, honest reporting.

Posting the Pillars

Across the country, the nuclear navy prominently posts Rickover's principles of watchstanding in its centers, offices, and ships. Every person, from the commodore down to the newest recruit, knows them and has them ingrained.

We have the opportunity to do the same with the five pillars in healthcare. Through computer screens, in workspaces, and on digital learning boards, we ought to post the five pillars as constant reminders of what is expected. Every single healthcare worker should have the five pillars tattooed on their mind and heart. Without them—without backup, formality, and all the rest—mistakes will be made to begin with, and sustainment will be lost in the end.

Safety Surveys

Another proactive tool organizations have for creating safer processes is surveys. Every year, all healthcare professionals working at a hospital should complete a culture-of-safety survey covering various domains. Each unit (ED, med/surg, ICU, ancillary, etc.) should receive scores from these surveys. Using those scores, the unit leader, collaborating with the patient safety champion, can identify an area of need and a plan of action for the team to focus on.

After a specified period has elapsed, follow-up surveys should be administered, designed to provide feedback and suggest a next area of focus. Such a process can help units improve performance in problematic areas and enable them to ensure that the same issues do not persist.

Coaching Sessions

Coaching is another way to achieve sustainment. At one point, we saw that the lessons some surgeons and other physicians learned already just weren't sticking. So, we began to coach them on developing healthy cultures and becoming more positive leaders.

One surgeon was on his ninth life. He verbally abused nurses and ancillary personnel often, and the med staff had to intervene more than once. Inevitably, the more they confronted him, the more defensive he became. The hospital felt reluctant to let the man go because he was an exemplary surgeon with incredibly high standards—and the turnover cost would be exorbitant. But no tools in the hospital's toolbox seemed to work on him.

When we became involved, we made it clear that we had come to help, not to get anyone in trouble. We listened to those on the receiving end of the surgeon's unprofessional behavior, as well as the surgeon's own concerns. We asked about the man's frustrations, barriers, and personal issues. We tried to get a complete picture of the causes behind the surgeon's unacceptable behavior.

After listening and helping both parties communicate their concerns with each other, we brainstormed with the surgeon on ways to build back trust.

It wasn't easy. This surgeon had so broken trust with his team that the hospital mandated he apologize to his staff. His apology would determine if he could stay at the hospital.

The surgeon felt raw from the med staff's continued interventions. He knew his head was on the chopping block, and he felt that apologizing would expose his neck even further. But we convinced him that the opposite was true.

In an effort to apologize authentically, the surgeon studied an article from Pepperdine University that discussed Nicholas Tavuchis's aspects of a genuine apology, taken from his 1993 book *Mea Culpa: A Sociology of Apology and Reconciliation.* Tavuchis said the offending party must:

1. Acknowledge through speech the legitimacy of the violated rule.
2. Admit fault for its violation.
3. Express genuine remorse and regret for the harm caused by the violation.[129]

The surgeon spoke to his team and took full responsibility for the situation, expressing his genuine regret for failing to care for them. His apology elicited a profound reaction. One person, who had deep empathy for the surgeon, left the room crying. The acute emotions of pain and relief the team displayed were similar to what you would expect from friends and family members of an addict fresh out of rehab.

Obviously, the story couldn't end there. The surgeon could not apologize and then return to his old ways. He needed to build upon and sustain the progress made. He had to address the issues causing his inappropriate behavior so he could rebuild trust with his work family.

Members of his surgical team began to meet to discover how to provide the tools the surgeon needed to enable him to focus on his patients. Expectations had to be clearly stated, and solutions had to be found for remaining barriers. In the beginning, the team's deep skepticism made the meetings tense. But, as issues were addressed and the surgeon's demeanor changed, the meetings became productive and even filled with laughter.

It's been three years since the surgeon's apology, and the newfound culture of professionalism has been sustained; he has continued to operate without a single professional complaint against him. The intervention redeemed the surgeon, revitalized his team, and served the many patients who benefitted from his clinical expertise.

The Core to Sustainment

Has a new system or procedure just been introduced to address an ugly baby? Great! What is the plan to keep it going? Who is going to check up on it and how often will they check?

Conversation-based rounds, FMEAs, audits and verifications, surveys, and coaching sessions all contribute to sustainment. But they are not the core of an HRO. High reliability in healthcare only occurs when an organization's strategy and culture align—when the five pillars of high reliability and such values as transparency and accountability permeate an organization.

18

FINAL THOUGHTS

Creeds aren't often a part of modern-day lingo. So, as we return to the five pillars at the close of this book and draw one last comparison between them and Weick and Sutcliffe's principles of high reliability, allow us to nerd out for a moment and step into the *Star Wars* universe to make what we believe is an apt comparison.

In *Star Wars,* the Galactic Empire is a powerful autocracy that has a canon of officially endorsed ideas by which it makes all its judgments. These principles are held to be incontrovertibly true, and the citizens and subjects of the Empire must submit to them. The Empire quickly stifles any objection to its way of doing things, which leads to its eventual collapse.

Not under the rule of the Empire, the Mandalorians are known for their independence, as well as their adherence to a common creed. The guiding values of the Mandalorian creed—such as loyalty, solidarity, and trustworthiness—allow for creative thinking within a proven, dependable framework. The expansive creed is far more productive than the limited canon of the Empire.

Do you see where we are going with this?

Time to Step Up

Weick and Sutcliffe's principles of high reliability have become healthcare's canon, its officially endorsed writings. But the belief in the incontrovertible truth of the principles has stifled new ideas, while the situation has grown increasingly worse.

More than ever today, we need strong, independent voices unafraid to question the dogma, individuals driven by conviction who wish to operate on different precepts that have the power to change the status quo for the better.

We need medical professionals ready to embrace a healthcare creed based on Admiral Hyman G. Rickover's watchstanding principles (the five pillars). Such a creed would guide every professional's action and remain in the thoughts and conversations of everyone involved in every aspect of healthcare. It might read something like this:

> I work in healthcare because I want to bring healing, hope, and strength to my patients.
>
> I work to gain a higher level of understanding.
>
> I insist on having personal integrity.
>
> I work in a group that has organizational integrity.
>
> I follow formal communication and procedures.
>
> I have a questioning attitude.
>
> I accept backup, and I will forcefully back up my teammates.
>
> I live by this creed, not by clinging to a dogma or canon. And I believe that I can have a huge impact for good in my chosen profession.

Are you a healthcare Mandalorian? Have we convinced you that "this is the way"? Do you believe that, with the right strategy and culture, a committed, forward-thinking vanguard can finally make high reliability healthcare a reality? If so, we welcome you to join us. Because in healthcare, as in *Star Wars,* "rebellions are built on hope."[130]

Be a Change Agent

We need open-minded problem solvers at all levels of healthcare, whether frontline workers, support staff, or C-suite leaders. Each person can make a difference.

In some organizations, at some levels, it may feel impossible to influence change. If the CEO of a system, for example, is not willing to give more than lip service to high reliability healthcare, can individuals in various departments really take any kind of effective action? At times, it may feel discouraging and even unsafe to speak up.

We fully understand and appreciate such a perspective. But we also know that there are ways to speak up or effect change even in trying situations. A good place to start could be a culture-of-safety survey. These surveys help to identify safety concerns and, because they are generally expected and easy to perform, are not usually met with resistance.

Any leader at any level can make a big difference by creating a culture that insists, "Everyone here has a voice. They're listened to. They're part of a team that cares about them and fixes things."

Being a change agent is not easy or even common. In fact, it might feel like pushing against the tide. Though most healthcare systems talk about becoming HROs, the practices and decisions of many indicate that they are ruled by financial concerns.

In financial crises, public schools often cut art, music, and drama programs. Similarly, healthcare systems often cut safety and high reliability. We've seen it happen.

Safety Comes from Good Leadership

Regardless of current setbacks, some universal principles cross all industries, including the nuclear navy and healthcare. One of those principles is that safety flows from good leadership and good operations.

Safety and efficiency go hand in hand. Striving for both increases profits, decreases waste, fosters innovation, and leads to increased retention.

Good leaders engage their people, teaching every individual to believe they're making a positive difference. CEOs have the most power and influence in this sphere, but leaders at all levels can get the ball rolling.

Leadership is a contact sport. Healthcare needs CEOs and other top leaders to commit themselves to culture building, the five pillars, and the other competencies critical to an HRO.

We urge you to get out there and watch your teams work.

Institute safety huddles, executive safety rounding, and the many additional tools we've discussed to increase safety throughout your organization. Think about how you can disseminate important lessons quickly and keep the five pillars of high reliability at the forefront.

Be a support—not a roadblock—for your safety team, making it clear to all your staff and patients that safety and high reliability are the primary focus of your organization.

Celebrate your people for following the five pillars. Encourage them to speak up and share their mistakes and lessons learned throughout the organization—and externally, if possible.

Though progress may be gradual—case by case, unit by unit, hospital by hospital—we can know that we're demonstrating Rickover's "courageous impatience" and making progress in bringing health, hope, and strength to more and more patients.

And isn't that worth the fight?

EPILOGUE

POWER TO CHANGE

We opened this book with the story of nurse RaDonda Vaught and a medication error that cost a patient her life. A failure of formality, understanding, organizational integrity, and backup all contributed to the tragic event. As we end, we'd like to tell a story about another medication error. This one could have also proven fatal and affected far more patients. It *could* have, but it didn't.

A technology update to our system left a few bugs in its wake, as technology updates often do. Unnoticed at first, the update somehow impacted the instructions for a particular pediatric chemotherapy drug, changing the directions for administering it from oral to intravenous. The altered, incorrect instructions went out to every campus within the system. If anyone even noticed the instructions had been changed, they probably assumed that the switch had come from the drug's manufacturer. In any case, no one spoke up. That is, no one but a pediatric pharmacist named Jonathon. Jonathon was sure the medication in question was meant to be given orally and believed it would be deadly if given intravenously. Rather than assuming the manufacturer had made a change, Jonathon picked up the phone to confirm. As soon as he established that the drug was *not* to be given intravenously, he notified his campus's safety supervisor, who then disseminated the information throughout the system. Jonathon had caught the mistake within twelve hours, before the medication had been administered to any patient at any facility in the system.

Shortly thereafter, we held our first Speak Up for Safety event, and shared pharmacist Jonathon's story. His incredible catch potentially saved the lives of many children. We celebrated his formality, his higher level of understanding, his integrity, and especially his questioning attitude. He was also empowered to speak up because he had a caring supervisor who made him feel safe to do so. Jonathon's story inspired many throughout the system to have questioning attitudes and led to the reporting and resolution of other safety issues.

Though he was just one individual, acting in accordance with the five pillars of high reliability, Jonathon made an extraordinary, life-saving impact. That's the power of the five pillars, and the power of each person.

ACKNOWLEDGMENTS

Jeffrey Kuhlman

This book will ruffle the feathers of many healthcare leaders. It may disrupt their thinking and comfort level. Healthcare is delivered to one human at a time by a team of professionals working together. In putting "pen to paper" and writing this book with Navy Bob, he has taught me, and I have learned a tremendous amount—not just about healthcare but also about life.

Thank you to my generation next—Michael and Jolie, Isabella and Daniel, Lena, and Henry—for helping me have a higher understanding of what life is about, learning that integrity is living your life the right way regardless of whether anyone is watching, having appropriate formality and respect in communication with each other, maintaining a questioning attitude and healthy skepticism about life, and above all, backing each other up!

Thank you most of all to my life partner, Sandy Montaperto Kuhlman, who is the most reliable person I know.

Robert Roncska

To my wife of over thirty years, Stephanie, thank you for bringing it all together and for being my sounding board. I love you more than anything. You have always been there for me and continue to support my dreams and goals to help others.

Next, I'd like to thank my children, Sophia and Zack, for the sacrifices you made by allowing me to pursue a military career, for standing strong through moves and deployments, and for tolerating me as I went back to school. I missed out on quite a few birthdays, holidays, and sporting events, but you remained supportive and understanding. I can't express how proud I am of both of you!

My healthcare journey would not have been possible without the love and support of so many. Thank you, Dr. Jeffrey Kuhlman and Dr. Dave Moorhead, for starting me on the path and Dr. Neil Finkler for guiding me as I went. Thank you to my safety team, Karina Coapstick, Jaclyn Jeffries, Tania Aylmer, Sam Miller, Grace Lai, Sharon Edwards, Teresa Tomlinson, Kya Andrews, Lauryn Verica, Soryda Rodriguez, Nicole Sneed, and Angela Victor, who went into the healthcare battle with me. We made a difference in the lives of so many.

Finally, I'd like to thank our editor, Stacey Tol, and ghostwriter, Steve Halliday. Stacey and Steve, you are an inspiration, and I'm so grateful for your expertise.

ABOUT THE AUTHORS

Jeffrey "Leno" Kuhlman

Jeffrey Kuhlman served as a navy physician for thirty years. He also spent sixteen years supporting presidents Clinton, Bush, and Obama as Marine One flight surgeon, White House physician, Camp David physician, flight surgeon aboard Air Force One, and director of the White House Medical Unit. When covering the president, Dr. Kuhlman was never further than two minutes from him. In this role, he gleaned personal lessons about the importance of information and relationships built on trust.

As physician to the president, Dr. Kuhlman coordinated comprehensive healthcare for the president and first family in addition to overseeing medical care for the vice president (and family) as well as for senior White House staff and Cabinet members. He was also responsible for emergency medical actions and advanced contingency planning, which necessitated collaboration of the White House Medical Unit with the Secret Service protective details. Dr. Kuhlman provided guidance and advice on all joint service, interagency, and international matters for medical contingency planning and operations. Additionally, he traveled to more than ninety countries to review their healthcare resources and protocols. His oversight even extended over force protection (preventive measures to mitigate hostile actions involving personnel, resources, facilities, and critical information), population health, and workplace health and safety programs for all workers and guests on the White House complex at home and abroad.

His mantra: "No policy, no politics—just trusted medical advice."

Dr. Kuhlman completed three board certifications: aerospace, family, and occupational medicine. In addition to being board certified in medical management, he is a certified physician executive by the American Association of Physician Leaders and a certified professional in patient safety. His global health expertise includes the certificate in travel health by the International Society of Travel Medicine.

Captain Kuhlman's hands-on experience in high reliability is based on his aerospace medicine expertise and operational assignments in naval aviation. This includes deployment on a nuclear-powered aircraft carrier, the USS *Enterprise* (CVN-65); assignment to Marine Aircraft Group 39; tour of duty with Naval Forces Europe; nineteen years as a navy flight surgeon; and designation as a senior aviation medical examiner for the Federal Aviation Administration.

Since 2013, Dr. Kuhlman has served as a chief medical officer and now as the chief quality and safety officer for AdventHealth, America's largest Protestant non-profit healthcare system, guiding quality, safety, and clinical transformation and teaching the pillars of high reliability healthcare.

Robert "Navy Bob" Roncska

Dr. Robert "Navy Bob" Roncska has an impressive background and a diverse range of experiences. He has held various leadership positions in both the military and civilian sectors, focusing on leadership, safety, health, and high reliability.

After retiring as a navy captain in 2018, Bob joined AdventHealth's Central Florida Division (CFD) South Hospital as the executive director for patient safety. He subsequently took on roles as the corporate executive director for high reliability and unit culture and later as the CFD radiation safety executive director. In these positions, Bob implemented best practices from his experience in the nuclear navy to improve quality, reduce harm, and promote transparency in patient care.

Bob also served as the senior vice president of the Florida Health Council at the Florida Chamber of Commerce. In this role, he led a 184 business-led health initiative to develop local behavioral health systems, implemented best practices, and created a model of mental well-being outcomes that can be replicated nationally. Currently, he is an adjunct professor at the University of Central Florida School of Global Health Management and Informatics, where he teaches graduate students.

Prior to his civilian career, Bob had a distinguished twenty-eight-year career in the US Navy. He served as the Pacific Fleet's top fast-attack submarine commodore, overseeing ten Los Angeles-class nuclear submarines and leading over 1,700 personnel with assets and a budget exceeding twenty-five billion dollars. In this role, Bob was responsible for overseeing numerous unprecedented missions vital to national security. While acting as the commanding officer of the USS *Texas* (SSN 775), a Virginia-class fast-attack nuclear submarine, he completed multiple deployments and conducted the first Virginia-class submarine arctic certification. Under his leadership, the USS *Texas* received accolades, including the best-performing ship award in the squadron, and had the highest personnel retention and lowest attrition in the Pacific Fleet for two consecutive years.

Bob's military career also included serving as the naval aide to President George W. Bush, a role in which he was responsible for the safety of the Executive Office of the President and handled extremely sensitive national security programs while carrying the "nuclear football." He was warmly dubbed "Navy Bob" by the forty-third president, George W. Bush.

Bob holds an Executive Doctorate in Business Administration from the Crummer Graduate School of Business at Rollins College. He is married to his wife of over thirty years, Stephanie, and has two children, Sophia and Zachary. They currently reside in Winter Park, Florida.

* * *

"Leno" and "Navy Bob" got their nicknames from President George W. Bush when they served together as White House physician and military aide to the president for the final two years of his presidency.

ENDNOTES

1. “Former Tennesse Nurse RaDonda Vaught Found Guilty in Woman’s Death after Accidentally Injecting Her with Wrong Drug,” CBS News, March 29, 2022, https://www.cbsnews.com/news/radonda-vaught-nurse-guilty-death-charlene-murphey-wrong-drug/.
2. “RaDonda Vaught Homicide Case,” Wikipedia Foundation, last modified March 15, 2024, 02:20, https://en.wikipedia.org/wiki/RaDonda_Vaught_homicide_case.
3. Brett Kelman, “In Nurse’s Trial, Witness Says Hospital Bears ‘Heavy’ Responsibility for Patient Death,” *KFF Health News*, March 24, 2022, https://www.npr.org/sections/health-shots/2022/03/24/1088397359/in-nurses-trial-witness-says-hospital-bears-heavy-responsibility-for-patient-death.
4. Connor Lusk et al., “Reconsidering the Application of Systems Thinking in Healthcare: The RaDonda Vaught Case,” *British Journal of Anaesthesia* 129, no. 3 (September 2022): e61-2, https://doi.org/10.1016/j.bja.2022.05.023.
5. Linda T. Kohn, Janet M. Corrigan, and Molla Donaldson, eds., *To Err Is Human: Building a Safer Health System*, (Washington, D.C.: National Academies Press, 2000), https://www.doi.org/10.17226/9728.
6. “Report Highlights Public Health Impact of Serious Harms from Diagnostic Error in US,” Johns Hopkins Medicine news release, June 17, 2023, https://www.hopkinsmedicine.org/news/newsroom/

news-releases/report-highlights-public-health-impact-of-serious-harms-from-diagnostic-error-in-us.

7. David W. Bates et al., "The Safety of Inpatient Health Care," *The New England Journal of Medicine* 388, no. 2 (January 2023): 142-153, https://doi.org/10.1056/NEJMsa2206117.
8. Bates, "The Safety of Inpatient Health Care," 142.
9. Martin A. Makary and Michael Daniel, "Medical Error—the Third Leading Cause of Death in the US," *The BMJ* 2139 (May 2016): 353, https://doi.org/10.1136/bmj.i2139.
10. David W. Bates et al., "The Safety of Inpatient Health Care," *New England Journal of Medicine* 388, no. 2 (January 2023): 142-153, https://doi.org/10.1056/NEJMsa2206117.
11. Jannik Lindner, "Medical Billing Errors Statistics [Fresh Research]," GITNUX Market Data Report 2024, December 16, 2023, https://gitnux.org/medical-billing-errors-statistics.
12. Lisa O'Mary, "Misdiagnosis Seriously Harms 795,000 People Annually: Study," WebMD, July 19, 2023, https://www.webmd.com/a-to-z-guides/news/20230719/misdiagnosis-seriously-harms-people-annually-study.
13. Rayhan A. Tariq et al., "Medication Dispensing Errors and Prevention," StatPearls [Internet], May 2, 2023, https://www.ncbi.nlm.nih.gov/books/NBK519065/.
14. "10 Facts on Patient Safety," World Health Organization, August 26, 2019, https://www.who.int/news-room/photo-story/photo-story-detail/10-facts-on-patient-safety.
15. "Healthcare Research and Quality Act of 1999," Agency for Healthcare Research and Quality, last modified October 2014, https://www.ahrq.gov/policymakers/hrqa99a.html.
16. Institute of Medicine (US) Committee on Quality of Health Care in America, *Crossing the Quality Chasm: A New Health System for the*

21st Century, (Washington, D.C.: National Academies Press, 2001), https://www.ncbi.nlm.nih.gov/books/NBK222274/.

17. Karl E. Weick and Kathleen M. Sutcliffe, *Managing the Unexpected: Sustained Performance in a Complex World*, 3rd ed. (Wiley: Hoboken, NJ, 2015), 94.
18. "Lean Six Sigma," Wikipedia Foundation, last modified February 28, 2024, https://en.wikipedia.org/wiki/Lean_Six_Sigma.
19. "Hospital Accreditation Fact Sheet," The Joint Commission, accessed March 18, 2024, https://www.jointcommission.org/resources/news-and-multimedia/fact-sheets/facts-about-hospital-accreditation/.
20. "Who We Are," The Joint Commission, accessed March 29, 2024, https://www.jointcommission.org/who-we-are/.
21. "NIAHO Hospital Accreditation," DNV, accessed March 18, 2024, https://www.dnv.us/supplychain/healthcare/ac/.
22. "About Us," DNV, accessed Feb. 23, 2024, https://www.dnv.com/about/index.html.
23. "Our Organization," DNV, accessed Feb. 23, 2024, https://www.dnv.com/about/in-brief/our-organization.
24. "Welcome to PSCA," Patient Safety Coaches Academy, LLC, accessed March 18, 2024, https://www.patientsafetycoach.com/.
25. "Allan Frankel," The Org, accessed March 18, 2024, https://theorg.com/org/safe-reliable-healthcare/org-chart/allan-frankel.
26. "The Framework for High Reliability Healthcare," Safe & Reliable and Vizient (white paper), accessed March 31, 2024, https://info.vizientinc.com/framework-for-high-reliability-healthcare.
27. Kohn, Corrigan, and Donaldson, eds., *To Err Is Human.*
28. "Study Suggests Medical Errors Now Third Leading Cause of Death in the U.S.," Johns Hopkins Medicine News and Publications, May 3, 2016, https://www.hopkinsmedicine.org/news/media/releases/study_suggests_medical_errors_now_third_leading_cause_of_death_in_the_us.

29. Carlos A. Pelligrini, "Revisiting *To Err Is Human* 20 Years Later," American College of Surgeons, Feb. 1, 2020, https://www.facs.org/for-medical-professionals/news-publications/news-and-articles/bulletin/2020/02/revisiting-to-err-is-human-20-years-later/.

30. Pelligrini, "Revisiting *To Err Is Human* 20 Years Later."

31. Kohn, Corrigan, and Donaldson, eds., *To Err Is Human.*

32. Weick and Sutcliffe, *Managing the Unexpected*, 66.

33. Weick and Sutcliffe, *Managing the Unexpected*, 99.

34. Rajeev Rathi et al., "Lean Six Sigma in the Healthcare Sector: A Systematic Literature Review," *Materials Today: Proceedings* (abstract) 50 (2021), https://pubmed.ncbi.nlm.nih.gov/35155129/.

35. Mark Chassin, "One-Size-Fits-All Approach to Patient Safety Won't Achieve Goal," Modern Healthcare, November 19, 2019, https://www.modernhealthcare.com/opinion/one-size-fits-all-approach-patient-safety-wont-achieve-goal.

36. Mark Chassin, "Patient Safety Leader Reflects on *To Error Is Human* Report," Advancing Health: A Podcast from the American Hospital Association, November 13, 2019, 32:49, https://www.aha.org/advancing-health-podcast/2019-11-13-patient-safety-leader-reflects-err-human-report.

37. Younis Munshi et al., "Leeching in the History—a Review," *Pakistan Journal of Biological Sciences* 11 no. 13 (July 2008): 1650-53.

38. Jessica Martucci, "Medicinal Leeches and Where to Find Them: The Rise, Fall, and Resurrection of the Humble Leech," *Distillations Magazine*, March 24, 2020, https://sciencehistory.org/stories/magazine/medicinal-leeches-and-where-to-find-them/.

39. Martucci, "Medicinal Leeches and Where to Find Them."

40. Martucci, "Medicinal Leeches and Where to Find Them."

41. Martucci, "Medicinal Leeches and Where to Find Them."

42. Munshi et al., "Leeching in the History—a Review," 1650-53.

43. Subramanian Senthilkumaran et al., "Unexpected Reach of a Leech," *Journal of Parasitic Diseases* 37 no. 2 (October 2013): 291-93, https://doi.org/10.1007/s12639-012-0166-4.
44. "How Leeches Can Save Lives and Limbs for Some Patients," University Hospitals, March 23, 2020, https://www.uhhospitals.org/blog/articles/2020/03/how-leeches-can-save-lives-and-limbs-for-some-patients.
45. "About Us," Biopharm Leeches, accessed March 29, 2024, https://www.biopharm-leeches.com/.
46. "The Death of George Washington," American Eras, Encyclopedia.com, March 18, 2024, https://www.encyclopedia.com/history/news-wires-white-papers-and-books/death-george-washington.
47. "The Death of George Washington," Encyclopedia.com.
48. "Hyman G. Rickover," Wikipedia Foundation, last modified February 18, 2024, https://en.wikipedia.org/wiki/Hyman_G._Rickover.
49. Theodore Rockwell, *The Rickover Effect* (Lincoln, NE: iUniverse, Inc., 1992/2002), 24.
50. "Hyman G. Rickover," Wikipedia Foundation.
51. "The Man in Tempo 3," *Time*, January 11, 1954, accessed Feb. 21, 2024, https://content.time.com/time/subscriber/article/0,33009,819338-3,00.html.
52. "Hyman G. Rickover," Wikipedia Foundation.
53. Rockwell, *The Rickover Effect*, 56-57.
54. "Submarines in World War II," National Park Service, last modified July 8, 2022, https://www.nps.gov/articles/000/submarines-in-world-war-ii.htm.
55. Dwight D. Eisenhower, "Atoms for Peace," International Atomic Energy Agency, December 8, 1953, https://www.iaea.org/about/history/atoms-for-peace-speech.
56. Rockwell, *The Rickover Effect*, 122-23.

57. "Soviet Atomic Bomb Project," Wikipedia Foundation, last modified March 13, 2024, https://en.wikipedia.org/wiki/Soviet_atomic_bomb_project.
58. Hyman G. Rickover, "Doing a Job," GovLeaders.org, 1982, https://govleaders.org/rickover.htm.
59. Tom Sherwood, "Sherwood's Notebook: The Bureaucracy Issue," NBC 4 Washington, January 28, 2015, https://www.nbcwashington.com/news/local/sherwoods-notebook-the-bureaucracy-issue.
60. Kennedy Hickman, "Cold War: USS *Nautilus* (SSN-571)," ThoughtCo., April 5, 2023, https://www.thoughtco.com/uss-nautilus-snn-571-2361232.
61. Hickman, "USS *Nautilus*."
62. "Hyman G. Rickover," Wikipedia Foundation.
63. Rockwell, *The Rickover Effect,* 11.
64. Rockwell, *The Rickover Effect,* 19.
65. S. L. Greenslade, ed., *Early Latin Theology, Library of Christian Classics V* (Louisville, KY: Westminster Press, 1956), 36.
66. "Department of the Navy FY 2022 President's Budget," America's Navy, May 28, 2021, https://www.navy.mil/Resources/Blogs/Detail/Article/2638885/department-of-the-navy-fy-2022-presidents-budget.
67. "US Total Military Personnel Navy FY 2022-2024, by Rank," Statista, November 3, 2023, https://www.statista.com/statistics/239345/total-military-personnel-of-the-us-navy-by-grade; "United States Navy Reserve," Wikipedia Foundation, last modified March 22, 2024, https://en.wikipedia.org/wiki/United_States_Navy_Reserve.
68. Hope Seck, "Active Ships in the US Navy," Military.com, June 23, 2021, https://www.military.com/navy/us-navy-ships.html.
69. "Why the American Healthcare System Underperforms," The Peter G. Peterson Foundation, July 31, 2023, https://www.

pgpf.org/blog/2023/07/why-the-american-healthcare-system-underperforms.

70. "Fast Facts on U.S. Hospitals, 2024," American Hospital Association, last modified January 2024, https://www.aha.org/statistics/fast-facts-us-hospitals; Jenny Yang, "Number of Hospital Beds in the U. S. 1975 to 2022," Statista, July 31, 2024, https://www.statista.com/statistics/185860/number-of-all-hospital-beds-in-the-us/.
71. "Fast Facts: U.S. Health Systems Infographic," American Hospital Association, last modified April 2024, https://www.aha.org/infographics/2021-01-15-fast-facts-us-health-systems-infographic.
72. "Total Number of Active Physicians in the U.S., as of January 2024, by State," Statista, accessed March 24, 2024, https://www.statista.com/statistics/186269/total-active-physicians-in-the-us/; "Who Are Our Health Care Workers?" United States Census Bureau, last modified June 7, 2023, https://www.census.gov/library/stories/2021/04/who-are-our-health-care-workers.html.
73. Daniel Edelson, "4,539 Soldiers, Dozens of Fighter Planes: The USS *Gerald R. Ford* Arrives in Israel," Ynetnews, October 12, 2023, https://www.ynetnews.com/article/sjaz11hhbp; "USS *Gerald R. Ford*," Wikipedia Foundation, last modified March 22, 2024, https://en.wikipedia.org/wiki/USS_Gerald_R._Ford.
74. Carly Behm et al., "100 Largest Hospitals and Health Systems in the US," Beckers Hospital Review, last modified December 15, 2023, https://www.beckershospitalreview.com/rankings-and-ratings/100-largest-hospitals-and-health-systems-in-the-us-2023.html.
75. Peter Suciu, "The Boomin Beaver Is the U.S. Navy's Smallest Ship," *The National Interest*, August 28, 2020, https://nationalinterest.org/blog/buzz/boomin-beaver-us-navy%E2%80%99s-smallest-ship-167855.
76. "History," Grace Cottage, accessed March 29, 2024, https://grace-cottage.org/about-us/our-hospital/history/.

77. Terri Heimann Oppenheimer, "The Top Bachelor of Science in Nursing (BSN) Program in Every State," nurse.org, September 12, 2023, https://nurse.org/education/bsn-programs-by-state/.

78. Andreas Kuersten, "The *Feres* Doctrine: Congress, the Courts, and Military Servicemember Lawsuits Against the United States," Congressional Research Service, last modified April 5, 2023, https://crsreports.congress.gov/product/pdf/LSB/LSB10305.

79. "Medical Malpractice Payouts by State 2025," World Population Review, accessed March 3, 2024, https://worldpopulationreview.com/state-rankings/medical-malpractice-payouts-by-state.

80. James N. Kurtessis et al., "Perceived Organizational Support: A Meta-Analytic Evaluation of Organizational Support Theory," *Journal of Management* (abstract) 43, no. 6 (2017): 1854-1884, https://doi.org/10.1177/0149206315575554.

81. Aaron De Smet et al., "'Great Attrition' or 'Great Attraction'? The Choice Is Yours," *McKinsey Quarterly*, September 8, 2021, https://www.mckinsey.com/capabilities/people-and-organizational-performance/our-insights/great-attrition-or-great-attraction-the-choice-is-yours.

82. "The CEO Must Be the Ultimate Architect of Any Culture Renovation. Example: Booz Allen," Culture Renovation, accessed March 24, 2024, https://culturerenovation.com/the-ceo-must-be-the-ultimate-architect-of-any-culture-renovation-example-booz-allen/.

83. Don Jernigan, *The Hidden Power of Relentless Stewardship* (New York: Rosetta Books, 2016), 236.

84. Jernigan, *The Hidden Power of Relentless Stewardship*, 54.

85. Philip Gordon Wylie, *Generation of Vipers* (New York: Farrar & Rinehart: 1942): 44, https://en.wikiquote.org/wiki/Philip_Wylie.

86. Paul Cantonwine, "Caught in the Leadership Paradox: Insight from Admiral Rickover," Nuclear Newswire, July 3, 2014, https://www.ans.org/news/article-1592/caught-in-the-leadership-paradox.

87. DJ Chuang, "Origin Story: Parable of the Three Bricklayers," @djchuang (blog), Nov. 23, 2021, https://djchuang.com/origin-story-parable-of-the-three-bricklayers/.

88. "Sentinel Event Statistics Released for 2015," *Joint Commission Perspectives,* April 2016, https://info.jcrinc.com/rs/494-MTZ-066/images/Sentinel39.pdf.

89. Nancy Fliesler, "I-PASS This Patient to You: Improved Hospital 'Handoffs' Cut Adverse Events by Almost Half," Boston Children's Hospital, December 2, 2022, https://answers.childrenshospital.org/i-pass-handoffs/.

90. Lisa DiBlasi Moorehead, "Make Time for a Time Out," The Joint Commission, June 6, 2022, https://www.jointcommission.org/resources/news-and-multimedia/blogs/ambulatory-buzz/2022/06/make-time-for-a-time-out/.

91. "NHE Fact Sheet," Centers for Medicare & Medicaid Services, last modified December 13, 2023, https://www.cms.gov/data-research/statistics-trends-and-reports/national-health-expenditure-data/nhe-fact-sheet.

92. "President Signs Patient Safety and Quality Improvement Act of 2005," Office of the Press Secretary (press release), July 29, 2005, https://georgewbush-whitehouse.archives.gov/news/releases/2005/07/20050729.html.

93. Rockwell, *The Rickover Effect,* 85.

94. Scott Simon and John Rettie, "Telling the Story of Krushchev's Anti-Stalin Tirade," NPR, *Weekend Edition Saturday* (transcript), February 25, 2006, https://www.npr.org/templates/story/story.php?storyId=5233399.

95. "Speaking Up About Patient Safety Requires an Observant Questioner and a High Index of Suspicion," Institute for Safe Medication Practices, October 10, 2019, https://www.ismp.org/resources/speaking-about-patient-safety-requires-observant-questioner-and-high-index-suspicion.

96. William Cooper et al., "Association of Coworker Reports about Unprofessional Behavior by Surgeons with Surgical Complications in Their Patients," *JAMA Surgery* 154, no. 9 (September 2019): 828-34, https://doi.org/10.1001/jamasurg.2019.1738.

97. Adam Grant, "The most dangerous voice in a meeting is the HIPPO . . .," LinkedIn, 2020, https://www.linkedin.com/posts/adammgrant_the-most-dangerous-voice-in-a-meeting-is-activity-6607988123680980992-Rtwf/.

98. Scott Mautz, "The Highest Paid Person in the Meeting Is the Most Dangerous Voice, According to Wharton's Adam Grant," *Inc.*, January 2, 2020, https://www.inc.com/scott-mautz/the-highest-paid-person-in-meeting-is-most-dangerous-voice-according-to-whartons-adam-grant.html.

99. Jens Rasmussen, "Human Errors. A Taxonomy for Describing Human Malfunction in Industrial Installations," *Journal of Occupational Accidents* 4, no. 2-4 (September 1982): 311-33, https://doi.org/10.1016/0376-6349(82)90041-4.

100. MaxHelp (@maxhelp), "We mistakenly sent out an empty test email to a portion of our HBO Max mailing list this evening…," Twitter, June 17, 2021, https://twitter.com/maxhelp/status/1405712235108917249.

101. AT&T Wireless, "OK: Surgeon," television commercial, December 29, 2018, https://www.ispot.tv/ad/IZ6U/at-and-t-wireless-ok-surgeon.

102. "RCA^2: Improving Root Cause Analyses and Actions to Prevent Harm," Patient Safety Network, June 24, 2015, https://psnet.ahrq.gov/issue/rca2-improving-root-cause-analyses-and-actions-prevent-harm.

103. Chanu Rhee et al., "Prevalence, Underlying Causes, and Preventability of Sepsis-Associated Mortality in US Acute Care Hospitals," *JAMA Network Open* 2, no. 2 (2019), https://jamanetwork.com/journals/jamanetworkopen/fullarticle/2724768.

104. "Sepsis Fact Sheet," Sepsis Alliance, accessed March 24, 2024, https://sepsis.org/wp-content/uploads/2019/08/Sepsis-FactSheet-v2.pdf.
105. Shankar Vedantam et al., "How a Theory of Crime and Policing Was Born, and Went Terribly Wrong," NPR Short Wave, November 1, 2016, https://www.npr.org/2016/11/01/500104506/broken-windows-policing-and-the-origins-of-stop-and-frisk-and-how-it-went-wrong.
106. Vedantam, "How a Theory of Crime and Policing Was Born."
107. "Swiss Cheese Model," Wikipedia Foundation, last modified Oct. 8, 2023, 11:56, https://en.wikipedia.org/wiki/Swiss_cheese_model.
108. Ben Evans, "Missed Warnings: The Fatal Flaws Which Doomed *Challenger*," Space Safety Magazine, accessed March 26, 2024, https://www.spacesafetymagazine.com/space-disasters/challenger-disaster/missed-warnings-fatal-flaws-doomed-challenger/.
109. "*Deepwater Horizon* Oil Spill Settlements: Where the Money Went," National Oceanic and Atmospheric Administration, last modified April 20, 2017, https://www.noaa.gov/explainers/deepwater-horizon-oil-spill-settlements-where-money-went.
110. *60 Minutes*, "2010: Blowout: The *Deepwater Horizon* Disaster," produced by Graham Messick and Solly Granatstein, aired May 16, 2010, on CBS, https://www.youtube.com/watch?v=XkGOukBrqgs.
111. Giuseppe Vetrugno et al., "Malpractice Claims and Incident Reporting: Two Faces of the Same Coin?" *International Journal of Environmental Research and Public Health* 19, no. 23 (December 2022): 16253, https://doi.org/10.3390/ijerph192316253.
112. "25 Strange Laws in the Orange State," CoverHound, accessed March 29, 2024, https://www.coverhound.com/insurance-learning-center/25-strange-laws-in-the-orange-state.
113. "The Nuclear Submarine," Submarine Force Library and Museum Association, September 29, 2017, https://ussnautilus.org/the-nuclear-submarine/.

114. MaxHelp, "We mistakenly sent out an empty test email . . ."
115. MaxHelp, "We mistakenly sent out an empty test email . . ."
116. MaxHelp, "We mistakenly sent out an empty test email . . ."
117. Doug Bonacum, "Doug Bonacum Describes How SBAR Solved an Important Problem He Was Seeing," Institute for Healthcare Improvement (interview), September 10, 2018, https://ihimedia.podbean.com/e/doug-bonacum-describes-how-sbar-solved-an-important-problem-he-was-seeing/.
118. "About the Leapfrog Group," The Leapfrog Group, accessed March 29, 2024, https://www.leapfroggroup.org/about.
119. Allison Shapira and David Horsager, "To Win Over an Audience, Focus on Building Trust," *Harvard Business Review*, March 9, 2022, https://hbr.org/2022/03/to-win-over-an-audience-focus-on-building-trust.
120. Richard Day and Ed Rogers, "Enhancing NASA's Performance as a Learning Organization," *Ask Magazine*, May 2013: 36-39, https://appel.nasa.gov/wp-content/uploads/2013/05/NASA_APPEL_ASK22f_enhancing.pdf.
121. "Safety Officer – Requirement: Is There a Requirement to Specify or Identify a Safety Officer?," The Joint Commission, last modified May 9, 2023, https://www.jointcommission.org/standards/standard-faqs/hospital-and-hospital-clinics/environment-of-care-ec/000001217/.
122. Anne-Marie Howell et al., "Can Patient Safety Incident Reports Be Used to Compare Hospital Safety? Results from a Quantitative Analysis of the English National Reporting and Learning System Data," *PLOS ONE* 10, no. 12 (2015), https://www.ncbi.nlm.nih.gov/pmc/articles/PMC4674095/.
123. "'The Buck Stops Here' Desk Sign," in *A Dictionary of Americanisms on Historical Principles*, edited by Mitford M. Mathews (Chicago: University of Chicago Press, 1951), 198-199, https://www.trumanlibrary.gov/education/trivia/buck-stops-here-sign.
124. Rickover, "Doing a Job."

125. "Procedure for Failure Mode, Effects, and Criticality Analysis (FMECA)," NASA, August 1966, https://ntrs.nasa.gov/api/citations/19700076494/downloads/19700076494.pdf.
126. Hyman Rickover, "Responsibility is a unique concept . . . ," A-Z Quotes, accessed March 29, 2024, https://www.azquotes.com/quote/1395486.
127. "Medication without Harm," World Health Organization, accessed March 29, 2024, https://www.who.int/initiatives/medication-without-harm.
128. Ronald A. Nosek, Jr. et al., "Standardizing Medication Error Event Reporting in the U.S. Department of Defense," *Advances in Patient Safety: From Research to Implementation (Volume 4: Programs, Tools, and Products)* (Rockville, MD: Agency for Healthcare Research and Quality, 2005), 361, https://apps.dtic.mil/sti/pdfs/ADA434765.pdf.
129. Lee Taft, "When More Than Sorry Matters," *Pepperdine Dispute Resolution Law Journal* 13, no. 1 (2013): 181-203, https://digitalcommons.pepperdine.edu/cgi/viewcontent.cgi?article=1241&context=drlj.
130. Sydney Odman, "'Star Wars': 20 Memorable Quotes from the Iconic Films," The Hollywood Report, June 19, 2023, https://www.hollywoodreporter.com/lists/best-star-wars-quotes/may-the-force-be-with-you-3/.